GOD AND THE WORLD
The Coherence of Christian Theism

GOD AND THE WORLD

The Coherence of Christian Theism

HUGO MEYNELL

London SPCK 1971

First published in 1971 by S.P.C.K.
Holy Trinity Church, Marylebone Road
London NW1 4 DU

Printed in Great Britain by
The Camelot Press Ltd,
London and Southampton

SBN 281 02617 3

CONTENTS

ACKNOWLEDGEMENTS vi

INTRODUCTION 1

1 GOD AND THE WORLD 9

2 GRACE 42

3 EVIL 64

4 MIRACLES 84

5 PRAYER 98

6 THE SOUL AND AFTERLIFE 111

7 CONCLUSION 122

APPENDIX
WHITEHEAD ON GOD AND THE WORLD 129

NOTES 135

BIBLIOGRAPHY 145

INDEX 151

ACKNOWLEDGEMENTS

Sections of this book have already appeared in *The Month* and *The Heythrop Journal*. They are reprinted here by kind permission of the editors of these journals.

My thanks are due to my wife and to John Hick, who have read through the manuscript and pointed out many errors and inconsistencies.

Thanks are also due to the following for permission to quote from copyright sources:

Hutchinson and Co. Ltd.: *God and Philosophy*, by A. G. N. Flew.

S.C.M. Press: *New Essays in Philosophical Theology*, ed. A. G. N. Flew and A. C. MacIntyre (contribution by Ian Crombie).

INTRODUCTION

This book is on the philosophy of religion, by which I mean the description, analysis, and criticism of the language and concepts of religion. It has been said that philosophy is "talk about talk"; in accordance with this definition philosophy of religion will be talk about religious talk. The special concern here will be that department of religious talk which deals with God and the world and their relation to one another. There are of course many conceptions of the philosophy of religion, such as the constructing of a new religion, theorizing about the nature and implications of religious experience, or proving or disproving the existence of God or the immortality of the soul. But my purpose is not so much constructive or revisionary as descriptive. To describe the nature and function of religious language as it is now is, after all, a necessary preliminary to revising or reconstructing it effectively.

The term "theology" may most usefully be reserved for the activity of deriving knowledge of God, or gods, or the divine, or what has to do with religion, from the sources of this knowledge, whatever they are. Some religions, though they have reached a level of intellectual articulation which is certainly "theological" in this sense, are specifically atheistic; examples are Theravada Buddhism and Jainism. In others, like that variety of Hinduism represented by the thought of Shankara and some of the Upanishads, one would be hard put to it to say briefly whether God is believed in or not. Theology presupposes at least that there are sources from which religious knowledge may be obtained. The philosophy of religion would discuss, *inter alia*, what is involved in this presupposition. Hence, while philosophy of religion is not theology, it is a necessary adjunct to it. It is concerned with improvement in the method of doing theology, if a valid theology is possible at all; if it is not, with showing why it is not. Some have argued, for instance, that all kinds of theology make false assumptions as to matters of fact; others, that theology is essentially invalid, since the concept of "God", along with other concepts used in theology, is incoherent.

"Apologetics" may be defined as the commending of a religion to those who do not adhere to it. As in the case of theology, philosophy of religion in the sense intended here is distinct from apologetics and yet necessary for it. This is because it is impossible honestly or effectively to commend a belief of any kind, religious or scientific or historical, without having some idea of what it means. It must also be said that religious apologists have a characteristic vice—that of reducing the content of belief to those aspects of it most likely to appeal to those to whom it is being commended.[1] Christian belief, for instance, includes, or at least is usually supposed to include, belief that the universe was framed for a purpose; and thus Christian apologists, in approaching those who are impressed by any evidence of purposiveness in nature, are inclined to exaggerate this aspect of Christian belief at the expense of the rest. Similarly, opponents of religion are most inclined to harp on those elements of belief which have the greatest *prima facie* implausibility or absurdity, especially outside their context in the system of belief as a whole. A philosophy of religion which is concerned primarily to describe and analyse religious beliefs, and only secondarily (if at all) to commend or attack them, is the best safeguard against both types of misrepresentation.

It is useful in this context to compare the philosophy of religion with the philosophy of science.[2] Hardly anyone supposes that the philosophy of science consists entirely or even chiefly of arguments to commend or attack science as such. The main emphasis is on examination of the nature of scientific theories and arguments, and on laying down criteria for distinguishing between good and bad ones. As a matter of fact, in the contemporary world the validity and usefulness of science as such are not questioned to the extent that the validity and usefulness of religion as such, or any particular religion, are. So perhaps there is some reason to expect more space to be devoted in a work on the philosophy of religion to the justification of religion as such, than to the justification of science as such in a work on the philosophy of science. But it would be a mistake to dwell too exclusively upon this aspect of the matter. Some presupposition about the nature of religious theories and arguments, after all, is necessary for any justification or invalidation of them to be possible.

In the case of some putative subjects of inquiry, it would now generally be held among educated people that reflection on their constitutive method and subject-matter, in the light of the rest of knowledge and common opinion, shows conclusively, or at least strongly suggests, that the very questions which were asked in them are ill-formed, giving rise inevitably to answers which are misleading or downright wrong. Astrology is a clear example of such a subject. It is evidently a waste of time to ask the question, "What bearing does the fact that I was born while the sun was in Aries have on my career?", if this fact has no bearing on my career whatever; or "By what process can this pound of lead be changed into a pound of gold?", if in fact there is no such process. There arises a strong suggestion of falsehood, and consequent misdirection of interest, from the very posing of such questions, quite apart from how they are actually answered. One may compare the question "Have you stopped beating your wife?", addressed to the man who has never in fact done such a thing; though its very form leads one to assume that the man concerned has been in the habit of beating his wife at some time or other. The "caloric" theory of heat, and the "phlogiston" theory in chemistry, are examples of terminologies which have crystallized an ineffective and misleading strategy of asking questions about the world. The point here is not so much that astrology and so on are certainly not valid sciences, and that the phlogiston and caloric theories are false, as that our contemporary culture assumes them to be invalid and false. Religious discourse, and with it the validity of the concept "God", is *sub judice* in a way that scientific discourse and astrological discourse, which serious-minded people are inclined to accept or dismiss without a great deal of palaver, are not.

The examination of religious concepts is rendered difficult by the very many senses in which religious terms are used. This applies particularly to the term "God" itself. Wittgenstein is supposed to have said, apropos of the question of God's existence, that people had meant so many things by the word "God" that, until some selection from among these was made, there was no point in even trying to answer the question. The solution which I shall adopt here is to select from among these meanings one which is sufficiently central to shed light on all the others. According to this criterion, it appears to me that the meaning of "God" in the Bible and the central tradition of Christendom is the most suitable. The question of the relation of this conception of God to others, such as the Great Designer, the philosophical Absolute, the *ens a se*, the God or gods of other religious traditions, and the object of religious experience or worship, is left open for the present; it is a disputed question in contemporary theology, and one to which we will have to return later on.

It may be asked whether religious propositions are similar in type to scientific propositions (verified or falsified, perhaps, by religious experience as opposed to observation of and experiment on the physical world); or whether they are more analogous to the propositions of morals, or of poetry. It seems evident that different people use religious language in different ways. But I assume here what I assume in relation to the concept of God: that there exists a central core of assumption about the significance of religious propositions, and their connection with other types of proposition, in relation to which more eccentric assumptions may be set out.

Many recent writers have made a thoroughgoing contrast between the meaning of religious statements on the one hand, and those kinds of statement which can be true or false in the normal sense on the other. In effect, they represent religious assertions as not stating (as they appear to be) what may or may not be the case, but as expressing the general attitude to life of those who make them. This has been a feature both of writers influenced by continental existentialism and of those who practise philosophy in the English manner. R. Bultmann is a representative example of the first class, R. B. Braithwaite of the second.

Bultmann[3] understands the Christian faith as described by the New Testament to consist of two radically different elements. On the one hand it involves acceptance of the Word of God which judges and forgives each man here and now, delivering him from the guilt of his past and offering him an authentic existence, free of pride and the illusion of self-sufficiency, in the future; and on the other, it involves assent to merely factual propositions about a mythical Son of God, that he "descended" to earth, performed actions contravening the laws of nature, physically rose from the grave, and will appear in the future with a convulsion of the elements. Faith in the latter sense, the belief that one highly improbable series of events happened in the past and that another is to happen in the future, is incompatible (he says) with acceptance of the world-view of modern science; fortunately this has nothing to do with faith in the former sense, which it is the proper task of the Church of today to proclaim. The historical Jesus is unique in that he was the original bearer of this liberating Word of God, which sets us free at every moment to exist authentically; also, in that proclamation here and now of the story of the crucifixion of Jesus is this liberating Word of God *par excellence.* However, faith in the proper sense is not concerned with the historical Jesus, but with the Christ, the Word of God, which confronts us here and now, bringing us the new life of authentic existence. Hence historical inquiry into the veracity of the Gospel record (about which Bultmann, as a distinguished New Testament scholar, is very sceptical) can have for him no bearing on faith properly understood.

Bultmann's views are expressed in a number of writings; Braithwaite's are set out with extraordinary conciseness and force in a single pamphlet, *An Empiricist's View of the Nature of Religious Belief.*[4] Braithwaite notes a special difficulty about religious statements: that while they appear to allude to matters of fact, no verification or falsification such as one would expect for statements of fact is available in their case. Also, religious statements are widely supposed to have consequences for morality, whereas it is a central doctrine of empiricism that no statement of value, whether relating to morals or aesthetics, can be entailed by any statement of fact. (If this were possible, one could construct a contradiction by simultaneously asserting some statement of the form "X is the case" and denying one of the form "Y is good" or "one ought to do Y". Since no such contradiction can be constructed, the supposition on which the alleged possibility of one is founded, that every value judgement is logically equivalent to some statement of fact, must itself be false.) Braithwaite resolves the dilemma by suggesting that religious statements are not, as would at first appear, statements of fact at all, but that they are self-commitments by those who make them to certain patterns of behaviour—in the case of Christianity, one characterized by *agape* or love. Since moral judgements themselves are expressions of such commitments, the connection between religion and morals now becomes clear. The religions do not differ from one another much in the moral policies of which they consist; their difference is in the "stories" by means of which their adherents commit themselves to these policies. "Story" is a technical term in Braithwaite's theory of religion, at once wider and narrower in meaning than the term as used in ordinary discourse; the "stories" characterizing Christianity are not only the stories (in the usual sense) about Jesus and other stories in the Bible, but also prayers, creeds, and other forms of discourse used by Christians in religious contexts. Braithwaite points out that the factual veracity of the Gospels has no vital bearing on Christianity as he conceives it—though he remarks on the implausibility of the claim that they are entirely legendary. He further comments that such a remark as "I believe in God, but intend to lead as selfish a life as possible", while it is immoral or imprudent on the old view (by which religious statements are supposed to state facts of a special kind), is logically incoherent on his own; since the man who makes it is at once committing himself to and dissociating himself from that way of behaviour which is the very essence of Christianity.

It is remarkable that these two views of the nature of Christianity, for all the very different terms in which they are couched and philosophical traditions on which they draw, have so much in common with one another. Both reject as inessential to Christianity those beliefs about the past and expectations of the future which characterize faith according to the clear sense of the New Testament and the Creeds, and reduce it to our disposition to behave or feel in certain ways here and now. The underlying similarity of these two ways of thinking, for all their difference of expression, is demonstrated by their fusion in Paul van Buren's *The Secular Meaning of the Gospel.*

A third view, similar to these two in that it makes religious assertions independent of matters of fact in the usual sense, is attributable to C. G. Jung; it may be summed up in the dictum that religious statements are or may be "psychologically true". According to Jung, each of the great religions presents a picture of the dangers and difficulties of life in such terms that its adherents are helped to master them, or at least to endure them with reasonable calmness. Jung calls the great religions "psychotherapeutic systems", and evaluates them as such;[5] in their truth or falsity in any other sense, he does not seem interested, presumably because he regards the relevant questions as either meaningless or unanswerable. (His references to "metaphysics" in such contexts have the same derisive flavour as is to be found in the work of some recent British philosophers.) Now Jung's work is invaluable in the light that it throws on why the great religions, with the mythology and ritual which go with them, have the profound effect on human life that they do; and that religious statements and theories do have the function attributed to them by Jung, whatever other they may have, does not seem to me seriously disputable. But it is important that the question of the meaning of religious assertions, and of whether they are true or false, must not be confused with that of their psychological effectiveness as brought out by Jung and others.

It may easily be seen that each of these conceptions of religious or Christian language carries with it a characteristic understanding of the concept "God". For Jung "God" is that power which brings about the psychological adjustment of the individual; for Bultmann he is that which draws the individual out of inauthentic and projects him into authentic existence; while for Braithwaite the term "God" has a role in stories by which Christians and others commit themselves to their characteristic ways of life. In the traditional faith of Christians of all denominations God is all these things and more; also allegations of fact and way of life are inextricably linked together in belief in him. Expectations for the future, based on events believed to have happened in the past, make sense of present behaviour and profoundly affect present value-judgements. It seems to me that contemporary philosophers have made quite unnecessarily heavy weather of the question how hopes and fears about future matters of fact can make sense of present dispositions. A man who expects the resurrection of the dead and the life of the world to come, or a state of affairs in which the mourners will be comforted and the merciful obtain mercy,[6] will act in the light of this expectation, and many of his actions will only be intelligible in relation to it. A man's frenzied efforts to get out of a building, to take a parallel example, may seem quite senseless, until one knows that he expects the building to be a heap of smouldering rubble in five minutes. A tough programme of scholarly work, sustained at the expense of amusements or even of health, may seem senseless until one knows, say, that the man engaging in it has soon to take a difficult examination which will profoundly affect the subsequent course of his life. That a man should be exhausting himself by running down a street may seem pointless until one knows that he expects a train to leave the local station in a few minutes, and that he intends to catch it. He does not, as one would expect on the analogy of Braithwaite's theory, run down the street because it is part of a self-justifying moral policy, in which he encourages himself by a "story", the truth or falsehood of which is irrelevant, about a train leaving a station. The underlying logic of religious morality is fundamentally the same as it is in these commonplace examples; a man engages in a peculiar series of activities, which set the style of his whole life, because of what he believes to be the case and the bearing of this on his fate.

Traditionally, religious statements and theories have been regarded as having in common with scientific statements and theories that they are true or false. This is at least partly, as I shall try to show, because they have truth-conditions expressed in statements about the past and the future. By and large the theist differs from the atheist at least in that he has different expectations about matters of fact. To dispense with these, as Bultmann, Braithwaite, and Jung do in their analysis, is to reduce religious belief to subjective feelings or moral attitudes. Such analyses may enshrine useful suggestions as to how we ought to understand religious language *in future*; but they do not accurately represent any more than a restricted aspect of the meaning of religious statements as they *are* and *have been*. And it is these, and more especially the idea of God in relation to the world which goes with them, with which, for better or for worse, I shall chiefly be concerned here.

1 GOD AND THE WORLD

God as the Bible conceives him is only known and encountered in active relationship to the world. According to the biblical account, all that happens to (in the first instance) the Israelite nation, whether natural or historical events, is ascribed to the activity of God. He founded the nation as a race (Genesis), constituted it as a society by a mighty act of deliverance and the issuing of a code of laws (Exodus to Deuteronomy), punishes and comforts it by delivering it into the hands of its enemies and later rescuing it (Judges, Kings, the prophetic books), and promises a wonderful future destiny for it (Gen. 12.3; Mic. 4.2, 3). But the God of Israel, as is insisted more and more strongly in the later Old Testament period, is also the God of other nations, and looks after their destinies (Amos 9.7; Jonah 4.11); he brought mankind at large as well as Israel into being (Gen. 1.26). Not only the origins and vicissitudes of Israel and other nations, but those of the universe at large, are similarly ascribed to his activity (Ps. 29.1; Job Chs. 38—41). Other gods amount to nothing; they simply do not have to be reckoned with; they have no effective action on the world, and no control over the future (Isa. 41.21–4). But it is to and through Israel, and ultimately Christ and his Church as the new Israel, that God's purposes for the world and mankind are most fully and definitively revealed (Deut. 7.6; Zech. 14.16; Isa. 49.6).

It is certainly true that God's covenant with Israel, and later with the Church, is the primary focus of interest in the Bible, and his relationship with the world at large of comparatively peripheral interest. This has led some Christian theologians, notably Karl Barth, to hold that unless we begin with the assumption that it is the God of the covenant and the father of Jesus Christ who is also the creator and sustainer of the world, our very notions of "creating" and "sustaining" and of the God who creates and sustains, will be fundamentally wrong from the point of view of a properly Christian theology, which is as such based upon the biblical witness.[1] Yet it seems to me that there is no compelling reason why one should not come to an idea of God through his relationship to the world in general, and go on to say that "God" as so understood is he who has made a covenant with Israel and become incarnate in Jesus Christ. I may conceive of the postman first as "he who drops the letters in in the morning", and only later discover that this individual is also he who opens and shuts the post office and sells stamps there. Even if the latter aspects of his activity are those which engross most of my attention later on, this does not mean that my original way of identifying him was wrong as far as it went. At least, the relation of God to the world in general is the object of this study; and I am arguing that, even from the point of view of Christian theology, one can abstract from the fact that God has become incarnate in Jesus Christ, and not thereby make nonsense of the Christian concept of God itself. So I propose, as a preliminary definition of "God", *that which makes the things and brings about the events of which the world consists.* This, I would claim, accurately represents one aspect of the biblical account of who or what God is, though of course it by no means exhausts it. It has the additional advantage of corresponding to the notion of God held by Islam and many other non-Christian religions. This definition gives rise to special difficulties where the free actions of human agents are concerned; these will be dealt with in later chapters.

It would appear, from what I have said about God as the Bible conceives him, that God's being and nature, *that* he is and *what* he is, are known largely through his activities in the natural and human realms.[2] Some writers have claimed, however, that we have a more direct and immediate means of knowing him. Descartes argued in his second *Meditation* that each of us knows most certainly of his own existence, next that of God, and next that of the external world and other persons. Barth[3] has tried to claim, heroically, that the existence of God is the one matter of unconditional certainty for the man of faith, and that ultimately he is sure of his own existence, and that of the world, only by God's revelation. But better represented among Christian thinkers is that which corresponds, for better or worse, to contemporary common sense; that we are most immediately conscious of the existence of the material world and of ourselves within it, and of God secondarily and by way of his relation to the world and to ourselves. Arguments to God's existence from causality and dependence in the universe, and from design in the universe, all make this assumption. (These sorts of argument are what Kant summed up respectively in his "cosmological" and "physico-theological" argument.)[4] All of these remark on certain features of the world at large, and argue for the existence of God as alone accounting for the existence of a world with these characteristics. The "Five Ways" of Aquinas are outstanding examples of this type of argument. What is at issue here is not whether these proofs are valid or not, but the conception of God, and of his relationship with the world, which are implicit in the fact that they take the form that they do.

Those types of argument which try to prove the existence of God by showing that existence is part of the very definition of God, and hence that the statement "God does not exist" is a self-contradiction, are peculiar in that they do not depend on God's relationship to the world. (These are what Kant called the "ontological" argument; I shall call them arguments from mere definition.) These arguments are purely a matter of conceptual analysis, and have no bearing whatever on how we find things to be in the world. On the other hand, arguments from design, which invoke God to account for otherwise unaccountable adjustments of means to ends in the world, are a purely empirical matter. Arguments from causality and dependence are half empirical and half conceptual. One might put it that arguments from design treat the claim that God exists as a mere matter of fact that might or might not be the case, of the same order as the claim that there are grebes with red necks or that there is at least one metal which is liquid at normal temperatures. On the other hand, arguments from mere definition and from causality and dependence treat the question of God's existence rather on the analogy of such questions as whether minds exist or material objects exist; once you know what is meant by "material object" or "mind", it is odd to doubt that such things exist, since assumption of their existence is so inextricably tied up with our whole way of looking at the world. Similarly, these arguments suggest, once you really have a clear idea of what is meant by the term "God", you cannot seriously doubt that God exists. Arguments from causality and dependence mean by "God", in the first instance, the being who is related to the world of our experience somewhat in the way that I outlined above, as its "first cause" or "sufficient reason", and try to show that such a being must exist, given the existence of the world as we have it. The argument from mere definition goes further; not only is the assertion "God does not exist" obviously wrong, in the kind of way that the assertions "material objects don't exist" and "minds don't exist" are obviously wrong; it is actually self-contradictory. In my opinion it is at once the charm and the fallacy of arguments from mere definition that they take advantage of the apparent similarity between "The assumption that there exists an object corresponding to concept X is inextricably involved in our whole way of making sense of the world, and therefore X must exist", and "The meaning of 'X' is such that 'X does not exist' is actually self-contradictory".[5]

Kant complained of arguments from causality and dependence that they confused conceptual and empirical questions; yet many may feel that just this is their particular virtue, and that Kant's own philosophy treats empirical and conceptual questions as much more extricable from one another than they really are. The question of whether the General Theory of Relativity is true involves conceptual questions about the very nature of "space" and "time"; yet observed empirical facts may force one to adopt this particular theory, and all the revision of some of our most fundamental concepts which it entails, rather than the traditional scheme in terms of which notions like "absolute rest" and "simultaneity at a distance" made unequivocal sense. Questions like that of the existence of a stable ether through which light travels involve not just particular observable facts, though some of these will certainly be relevant, but the appropriateness of a whole way of looking at phenomena. The existence of God, like the existence of phlogiston or electrons, and unlike the existence of green hoopoes or graminivorous reptiles, is not a hypothesis that can be entertained on the assumption that, if it is true, the world at large remains just the same as if it were false.

Polemic against belief in a "God out there"[6] is presumably polemic against the conception of God as just one object among others, who might or might not exist as egg-laying mammals or goldfish over a foot long might or might not exist. The paradigm cases of "out there" existence are evidently particular instances and kinds of material object, the question of the existence of which is always a straightforwardly empirical one. Belief in the God who is the "source, ground, and goal" of our existence, on the other hand, is not so plainly an empirical matter. This conception of

God seems to be closer to the biblical one, and also to that of traditional Christian theology. Indeed, the second, third, and fifth of Aquinas' well-known Five Ways[7] of proving the existence of God seem to be summarized in this formulation of Bishop Robinson's; depending as they do on the idea of God as the source (that without which they would not have come into existence), the ground (that without which they would not remain in existence), and the goal (that without which they would not come to their final fulfilment) of all things that are not God.

But of the Five Ways of Aquinas, the first, which regards God as the source of change in the universe, seems to correspond most closely to the biblical view of him. It may be thought to depend on notions derived from Aristotelian philosophy, and so in a sense it does; but there are interesting parallels in contemporary thought. Aristotle's notions of "mover", "thing-in-potency" and "thing-in-act" are parallel to the "operator", "operand", and "transform" of contemporary cybernetics. The mover is what changes the thing-in-potency into the thing-in-act, as the operator is what changes the operand into the transform. In the first chapter of his *Introduction to Cybernetics*, W. Ross Ashby writes,

> Our first task will be to develop this concept of "change" . . . Consider the simple example in which, under the influence of sunshine, pale skin changes to dark skin . . . That which is acted on, the pale skin, will be called the operand, the factor (sc. in the sunshine) will be called the *operator*, and what the operand is changed into will be called the transform. The change that occurs . . . is the transition.[8]

It is evident that this schema can be applied to any number of examples, from the simple to the most complex. Indeed, cybernetics has in common with Aristotle's metaphysics that it has been developed specifically to cope with things at a higher level of generality than is done by the individual branches of science. One may find examples of transitions in blocks of wood, living organisms, colonies of organisms, individual men, families, factories, nations, or civilizations. An acorn is an operand with respect to an oak-tree as its transform, and the various chemical forces in the soil which in acting upon the acorn enable it to grow are the operator. An agricultural economy may be operand in a transition of which an industrial economy is the transform. A war may be the transition in which a group of nation-states is turned into an empire or the sphere of influence of a single powerful nation-state. Now it has often been pointed out that one great advantage of the philosophy of Aristotle, as against that of most of his predecessors and very many of his successors, is that it takes account of the phenomenon of change. Since Aristotle's philosophy and contemporary cybernetics are both preoccupied with the problem of change, it is perhaps only to be expected that there would be some resemblance between their ways of explaining the phenomenon; what is remarkable is the exactness of the equivalence. It is consequently very easy to translate into the terms of cybernetics the relationship between God and the world that has been set out by those philosophers who have applied Aristotelian terminology to the explanation of the biblical revelation.

If we mean by "nature" the aggregate of all the operators, operands, and transforms there are, have been, or will be, distinctions have to be made between (*a*) what is operator only, (*b*) what is operator with respect to some transitions and operand or transform with respect to others, and (*c*) what is operand or transform only. I cannot think of anything that could confidently be included in the last category; pure operand would be the mere capability of being changed into something, pure transform the mere possibility of having something changed into it. The things in the universe which exercise influence on one another and are affected by one another in various ways and to various degrees are both operators and operand-transforms; they both act and are acted upon.

Only God, as that which acts but is not acted upon, comes into category (*a*). If the causal arguments for God's existence, and the causal explication of the way he is related to the world, are understood in this sense, a whole series of misunderstandings may be swept away. There is no need to be perplexed, for example, by Hume's analysis of cause in terms of the constant conjunction of similar things and events. As Hume sees it, it is intrinsic to causal reasoning that we can properly infer that X is the cause of Y only when we have observed many instances of a thing or event of type X being succeeded by a thing or event of type Y;[9] hence, since we have not observed gods bringing universes into being, we have no valid grounds for holding that this universe has been brought into being by a god. But this kind of objection simply does not apply if causality is understood in the way I have outlined. Of the Five Ways of Aquinas, the first is the most directly relevant to cybernetics. To call God prime mover is to say that, taking nature as a whole as the system under discussion, God is operator, the present state of affairs among beings subject to change the operand, and any future state of affairs the transform. That God is *prime* or *unmoved* mover is that he is not operand or transform with respect to any operator, but always operator. That God is "pure act", without any admixture of potency, is that he is not operand with respect to any transform. Contingent beings are operands and transforms as well as operators; that they are dependent on God's operation for their existence and their own operation is what it is for them to be contingent. Nature is the system of systems; we say that God operates through secondary causes when a system and its changes can be accounted for as part of a larger system and its changes.

The coming of things into existence, as we are used to it in our dealings with the world, is nearly always a special instance of a thing or aggregate going through a process of change. Where wood is fashioned into a table, the table is brought into existence, but the wood, though changed, goes on existing; the chemical elements which make up any human body existed as such before they constituted that body, and do not cease to be themselves while they constitute it or after they stop doing so. This is as much as to say that the second Way of Aquinas, which argues to the existence of God as first in the order of "causes" in the limited sense of "cause" as that which brings things (substances) into existence, can be deduced from the first, and indeed regarded as a special instance of it. The same applies to the third Way, which contrasts that which is subject to change and decay (because it is operand with respect to transform) with that which is not (because it is operator only). The implications of Ross Ashby's terminology thus makes it clear why Aquinas himself thought the first way of paramount importance, and in the *Compendium Theologiae* claimed to deduce from it all the attributes describing from our point of view the essence of God.[10]

The concern of cybernetics is with operator, operand, and transform *qua* operator, operand, and transform—that is to say, in interaction with one another, and not in and for themselves. This is said by Ashby to apply particularly to the operator; ". . . though we may sometimes know something of the operator as a thing in itself (as we know something of sunlight), this knowledge is often not essential; what we *must* know is how it acts on the operands, that is, we must know the transformation that it effects."[11] This is presumably why Aquinas insists that God in natural theology (i.e. that independent of special revelation) is known only in his causal relationship to the world.[12]

Someone might raise the objection that on this view God is a *part of* nature, whereas according to all real theists he *transcends* nature. From the assumption that "nature" is all that exists, conjoined with the assumption that God transcends, i.e. is distinct from, "nature", of course God's non-existence can easily be seen to follow. This is the basis of what Professor Flew calls "the Stratonician presumption" of atheism.[13] The same dilemma, that God is either outside nature and so cannot exist, or is inside nature and so subject to empirical investigation and therefore not "God" in the proper sense, appears in a recently published dialogue.[14] And yet the equivocation underlying this false dilemma can easily be shown by the terminology I have introduced. The word "nature" can be used in three senses, to refer either to the system of all systems, or to all those operators which are also operands and transforms, or to that operator which is not operand or transform. In the first of these senses of "nature", God is a part of nature. In the second, he is unequivocally other than nature—he "transcends" it. In the third, he *is* nature. Professor Flew makes play with a dictum of Einstein about "the God who creates and is nature", alleging that Einstein thus evacuates the notion of "God" of its usual content.[15] But with the explanation that God *is* nature in the third of the senses of "nature" which I have outlined, and that he *creates* nature in the second, Einstein's formulation sounds to me as though it ought to be quite unexceptionable to the most conservative of theists.

The much-discussed question of God's immanence and transcendence, and the related problem of the sense in which God can be claimed to be "outside" or "above" or "beyond" the universe, becomes much easier to handle once the relation between the meanings of the terms "God" and "nature" is grasped clearly. An Old Testament scholar writes: "The Hebrew vocabulary includes no equivalent to our term 'Nature'. This is not surprising, if by 'Nature' we mean 'the creative and regulative *physical* power which is conceived of as operating in the physical world and as the immediate cause of all its phenomena'. The only way to render this idea into Hebrew would be to say simply 'God'."[16] This expresses very well, apart from the word in italics, the sense in which God *is* nature. A recent dictionary definition of "nature" brings out the crucial differences of meaning in the word (the italics are mine):

A collective abstract term for the entire universe, and embracing all its existences, forces, and laws, regarded as constituting a system or unity which may be covered, however vaguely, by one conception and designated by a single term. In this meaning, however, we are obliged to recognize an attempt to blend *two aspects or ways of regarding the universe* which are more or less distinctly different, while both are necessary. These are: (*a*) The system of things and persons regarded as actually existent *in space and time* . . . (*b*) The moulding or creative forces; the powers which account for the origins and changes of things, and for the production and evolution of the world in accordance with some . . . plan or controlling ideas.[17]

Given perhaps a substitution of singular for plural in "forces" and "powers", (*b*) is an excellent definition of "God" as understood by Christian, Jewish, and Islamic theists.

The importance for theism of conceiving clearly how "God" on the one hand, and "the universe" or "the world" or "nature" on the other, are supposed to be related, is illustrated by this crucial passage from Flew:

What the theologian needs is somehow to show how they [sc. the terms of the theologian's subject] can have, and have, application: and that in their most distinctively theological employments. The present case of terms such as *outside*, *inside* and *beyond* [sc. in expressing how God is supposed to be related to the world] is one of many examples good for illustrating his difficulties . . . The theologian wants somehow to direct attention away from the universe and towards what is thought to be outside, beyond, above or below. Yet all these prepositions are given their original meanings by reference to spatial relationships: this is outside that; that is beyond and above the other; which in turn is below some third thing. Clearly none of these literal senses can apply in the present case. Any thing or place which is in spatial relationship with any thing or place in the universe thereby becomes part of the universe . . . So it must be in a non-literal sense. Nothing in itself is wrong with that: all these terms already have plenty of non-literal senses. But what sense?

Presumably such that God is other than the universe; no other alternative seems to be offered or indeed open. But "the other, when what is not the other is the universe, is hard to identify as anything but nothing."[18]

Flew's argument here seems to be divisible into four main steps: (*a*) God cannot be literally "above" or "beyond" the universe; (*b*) the only intelligible non-literal sense in which God can be said to be so is that he is other than the universe. (*c*) But *prima facie*, at least, "the universe" *means* "all that exists"; (*d*) so it seems that nothing can exist which is other than the universe. The theist may concede the first two points, but need have no difficulty in rebutting the other two; he may simply introduce the definition of God I suggested earlier as that which performs all the events which happen and brings into being all the (other) things that exist. God is outside, above, below, or beyond the universe, in the sense of *all else* that exists, in that he brings it into being and sustains it in being by his activity, but is not *part of* it as so conceived. (The point at issue here, it is worth noting, is not whether God as so conceived can be *proved* to exist, but whether one can get a clear idea both of what is meant by "God", and of the sense in which this "God" is supposed to transcend or be other than the universe.) It seems to me that this idea of God is not only perfectly coherent, but that it also corresponds to what most theists, whether simple or sophisticated, have meant by the term "God". And yet, oddly, Flew's book devotes very little attention to it.

To be a pantheist is to confuse the agent with the results of his actions, to confuse that which is operator only with that which is also operand and transform. In Professor F. Hoyle's *Frontiers of Astronomy* there is described "a Universe in which the individuals —the clusters of galaxies—change and evolve with time but which itself does not change . . . Every cluster of galaxies, every star, every atom had a beginning, but not the Universe itself. The Universe is something more than its parts. . . ."[19] It is, one would infer, pure operator as well as operator which is also operand and transform, necessary as well as contingent being, *natura naturans* as well as *natura naturata*. By "the Universe" it is clear that Hoyle means "nature" in the first sense of those I mentioned above; that aspect of the universe which is over and above the sum of the parts of the universe is simply God. In his contribution to a symposium,[20] Hoyle says that he believes in a God in the sense of an intelligence at work in nature, but then he qualifies this by saying that he means by "God" the universe itself rather than some being who transcends the universe. And yet the logic of his position in *Frontiers of Astronomy*, which in effect distinguishes that which exists eternally from the mere sum of those things which come into being and pass away, is theist rather than pantheist. This distinction between the eternal and the passing still holds, of course even if, as I believe Hoyle thinks in opposition to the partisans of the "big bang" theory of the origin of the universe, there has always been a universe consisting of things coming into existence and passing out of existence. As Aquinas points out, that God exists (that there is an operator which is not operand or transform), and that he is Creator of the world (that this operator has brought into existence and brings into existence operands and transforms), is independent of the question whether the world came into existence in time.[21]

Pascal asked what the God of Abraham, Isaac, and Jacob had to do with the God of the philosophers; and *a fortiori* one might wonder what he had to do with the God of the cybernetician. For the Christian faith to be true is for the transform of each man, if he accepts God's operation on him, to be a saint, into which God moulds him by means of the secondary causality of other men and material things; and for the transform of the world as a whole to be the Kingdom of God, the state of bliss in which evil and misery will be done away with (cf. Rom. 8.22; Rev. 21.4). Now if all the coming into being and perishing of the galaxies, stars, planets, and atoms which constitute the universe is conceived to be the result of the operation of God, then it is plain that this God is not perishable in the way that the results of his activity are so. If someone said "God will cease to exist, but everything else will go on just the same, next Monday", it would be evident that he did not know what is meant by "God". God is not perishable, in the way that the things that constitute nature are, because he does not, as they do, depend for his existence and activity on the existence and activity of anything else. That it is of the very essence of God, that he does not come into being or pass away, that he is "eternal", is expressed poetically by, for example, Psalm 90, and in a different way by the metaphysical terminology of "necessary existence". To be a theist is to envisage the changing world as the working-out of the purposes of a being who does not change. The nature of this being is described in poetic and concrete terms by the biblical authors, but can be set out with greater precision and abstractness in terms of metaphysics on the Greek model. It has been suggested that it is an elementary error in the history of ideas to identify the metaphysical and the biblical conceptions;[22] but, if my reflections are correct, this aspersion is unfair. This is a matter of some importance, because the mainstream of Christian theology depends on the compatibility of Hebrew and Greek thought on this point. Both express, in their different ways, the eternity of God; for both, "God will have decomposed by tomorrow" is not just false, but senseless.

J. N. Findlay has complained that the existence of a being who has "an *unsurpassable* supremacy along all avenues", and who is such as to "tower *infinitely* above all other objects", is logically impossible; but he alleges that only such a being is an adequate object of religious devotion.[23] Yet it seems to me that God as I have described him, as that on whose existence and activity the existence and activity of all else depends, *is* exalted infinitely above all other beings and so is an adequate object of worship. But Findlay goes further, and says that a worthy object of worship must be such that its non-existence is inconceivable; in other words, such that it can be proved to exist by the argument from mere definition; and the idea of such a being, he says, is self-contradictory. But it is just this last quality, of having "necessary existence" in the sense objected to by Findlay, which I see no reason to attribute to a worthy object of worship, or to God as I have described him.

It is a commonplace that terms attributing qualities to God do not have precisely the same meaning as the same terms used to attribute qualities to men or things. Yet if the meaning of such terms is totally different in the two cases it is hard to see why one should not describe God with equal justification in any terms whatever. If, for instance, to say that God exists, or is powerful, or has knowledge, or is good, means something totally different from saying that a man exists, is powerful, has knowledge, or is good, one might just as well say that God does not exist, or that he is ignorant, impotent, or wicked. "We ought never to suppose", says Hume's Philo, "that his perfections have any analogy or likeness to the perfections of a human creature"; but to follow through Philo's recommendation consistently is to admit that whenever we say anything about God, we might just as well say exactly the opposite.[24] The advantage of the preliminary account I have given of who or what God is, is that it enables one to specify to whom or to what the terms ascribing the divine attributes are to be applied, and thus how the sense in which they are to be understood is related to the other senses of these terms.

If God does everything that happens, his power to act must be different not only in degree, but in kind, from that of anything else; since that anything else exists or acts at all is entirely due to God's existence and activity. God is omnipotent since, in virtue of what he is, nothing can resist his power, or occur absolutely against his will. (He may deliberately limit himself in some sense, where the action of rational agents is concerned;[25] but that is a different matter. The omnipotence of God has a bearing not on what he *will* do, but on what he *can* do.) As to omniscience: it might be asked on what grounds such a being, whose actions all events in some sense are, could be ignorant of anything. Human ignorance is a function both of the restrictedness of our field of action, and of the fact that the matter upon which we act is subject to forces beyond the control of our will, but God is not limited in either of these ways. As to how God can know eternally what depends on the free choice of rational agents, opinions differ. Some theists would say that there is no difference in principle between God's knowledge of what depends on free action on the one hand, and his knowledge of events which occur according to natural causality on the other. Others consider that one cannot accept this account of the matter without denying human freedom and responsibility, and would say that God has a special kind of knowledge of those future events which depend on the activity of free beings.[26] A very few theists have denied God's knowledge of the future acts of free beings altogether.[27] The question of what is meant by calling God "good", and of how his goodness is related to that of human beings and things, must be deferred until later.[28]

It may be asked what the notion of God which I have outlined has to do with religious experience, and argued that since religious experience is an important reason which many if not most theists have for their belief in God, my account of who or what God is supposed to be should have taken it into account. It is certainly true that what is called "religious experience" may lead a man to accept one general account of the world and man's place in it and to reject another, to see the world from a religious rather than from a non-religious or anti-religious viewpoint, and so to talk of events in terms of God's activity and purpose. But there are special difficulties and dangers in centring our conception of God on actual or alleged contact with him in "religious experience". It may easily lead to a conception of God as a mere internal accusative of verbs descriptive of religious experience, in such a way that "God exists" may seem to amount to nothing more than "certain psychological states may be achieved by some persons in some circumstances".[29] Whoever or whatever God is, the question of his existence, over which rivers of blood have flowed, can hardly be as trivial as this. Certainly impressive or awe-inspiring natural phenomena, the so-called "boundary-situations" of birth and death and tragedy, and perhaps above all contact with that outstanding moral or personal quality known as "sanctity" in other men (whatever relation the emotional impact of such things is deemed to have to that rather nebulous entity "religious experience"), often contribute to making men come to believe in God when they did not previously do so. Also, of course, they can have quite the opposite effect. In any case, as a basis for analysis of the concept God, they are insufficient.

The objections to a notion of God derived too exclusively from religious experience also apply to that which goes with existentialist conceptions of man such as that presented in Heidegger's *Being and Time*; the danger here is that God may be effectively conceived as active not in all events whatever, as in the biblical conception, but only in the move of the human individual from inauthentic to authentic existence. It is not being claimed here that these ideas of God based on religious experience and on existentialist anthropology throw no light on God as traditionally conceived; but only that, if taken as primary and determinative, they unduly restrict his being and activity. These notions are quite consistent with, and indeed may be derived from, the central biblical conception of God, since religious experience and the reorientation of human motives and behaviour are among the events and complexes of events which constitute nature at large; but the biblical notion is not subsidiary to and cannot be inferred from the existentialist one or that derived from religious experience.[30]

These two unduly restricted conceptions of God have been characteristically championed by theists; those which I shall now discuss are rather the preserve of atheists. Many atheists, in denying the existence of God, are denying the existence of a being who is needed on emotional grounds, as giving recompense to those who have been miserable in life, and as the wreaker of vengeance on their oppressors. The most influential of the atheists who have looked on God in this way, as essentially substitute gratification, are Freud and Marx. According to Marx, belief in God is an illusion evolved by men to make life tolerable in circumstances which are objectively intolerable, in which the struggle of society with its non-human environment is reflected by a still more crippling struggle within society itself. But man can now, by the technological means available to him, change his environment to suit himself, and can gradually acquire enough self-knowledge to abate the intestinal strife within society; therefore he has no need any more of the illusory comforts of religion. Not only is there no pie in the sky when we die, but the happy and fulfilled life possible for contemporary man makes it no longer necessary to hallucinate one.

Another version of the belief that theism is essentially substitute gratification is that of Freud. Freud's own view of the prospects of human life, as is well known, is one of profound pessimism. He had no more use for the Marxist utopia than for the Christian heaven. One might put it that for Marx the Christian heaven is objectionable because it stops men trying to bring about the one which is really obtainable; while for Freud all utopian hopes are based on the same false premiss, that is, that advances in civilization and raising of the general level of human happiness do not have to be paid for. Civilization, says Freud, does and must subsist at the price of the renunciation of a large number of instinctual gratifications, for which everyone more or less consciously hankers. The dilemma is unavoidable; either we follow the path of immediate gratification of our instincts, in which case our lives are dangerous and short; or we frustrate ourselves to some extent for the sake of security. Belief in God is one of several means, and according to Freud the least respectable, of reconciling ourselves to these frustrations. We comfort ourselves with the illusion that an omnipotent and loving being will recompense us for them with happiness here or hereafter. This belief derives in the first instance, he says, from the child's feeling of helplessness and its consequent longing for a father. "The whole thing is so patently infantile, so incongruous with reality, that to one whose attitude to humanity is friendly it is painful to think that the great majority of mortals will never be able to rise above this view of life."[31] What is even worse is that many educated people, whom one cannot believe themselves to be deluded, see fit to defend the illusion of religion by a series of rearguard actions, giving way only an inch at a time. More sophisticated and philosophical, and therefore less personal, notions of God, merely substitute sententious obscurity for crude wish-fulfilment.[32]

Freud's strictures are convincing in proportion to the degree of assent one accords to the basic assumption underlying them, that God is primarily or exclusively the offerer of consolation here and hereafter. But according to the central tradition of Christian doctrine, God is primarily he who has made the world and is transforming it into the kingdom of his Son, and who here and now lays upon each one of us a task within the fulfilment of this scheme; only *inter alia*, not primarily or exclusively, is he the giver of rewards and punishments in this life and the next. Not that the doctrine of a future life and of reward and punishment is not an essential *part* of Christian belief; the point is that Christian belief is not mainly or exclusively this. I believe that it is partly fear of criticisms like those of Marx and Freud that have led many recent theologians into underplaying these futuristic elements of Christian belief.[33]

Another conception of God often held by atheists is that of something invoked to explain the presence in the universe of an order such as is otherwise inexplicable. This is the God of the so-called "Argument from Design". The argument draws attention to the analogy between the universe at large and human artifacts in the adjustment of means to ends, and alleges that, since we assume that a designing intelligence has been at work in the production of artifacts, we ought to believe that the same is the case with the universe; and the designing intelligence which originally brought the universe into being is God. There are two typical forms of attack on the argument from design, which may be labelled the philosophical and the scientific. In Hume's *Dialogues concerning Natural Religion*, which is perhaps the classical discussion of the argument from design, the great disproportion in size between the universe and any human contrivance is stressed, and the consequent hazard of arguing from the known causes of the one to the unknown causes of the other. Also it is plausibly suggested by Hume that the world, or the small part of it with which men are acquainted, is just as analogous to an animal or vegetable as to an artifact. Thus, since animals and vegetables come into being as a result of procreation and seeding, we might just as well say that the universe came into being as a result of procreation or seeding rather than as a result of intelligent design—given that we are foolish enough to speculate on the origin of the universe as a whole on the basis of the infinitesimal knowledge of it that we possess.[34]

The scientific form of attack on the argument does not base itself on the general impropriety of arguing from what is true of tiny bits of the universe to what must be true of it as a whole; but merely asserts, surely rightly, that we now know to a large extent how such adaptation came about, that is to say, by random variation in inherited characteristics of organisms and natural selection; and hence that we no longer need the hypothesis of an intelligent designer to account for it. Nature is a self-supporting process, producing adaptations in organisms by random mutations and subsequent elimination of the maladapted. Hence there is no reason to believe in any supernatural adaptor. The most persuasive champion of this argument that I know of is Sir Julian Huxley, in his *Religion without Revelation.*

Huxley's conception of the alleged relation of God to the world is very odd, and seems to have much more reference to the God of the argument from design, the God of the seventeenth- and eighteenth-century Deists, than to the God of the Bible or the central Christian tradition. He seems to think that the admission that an event has happened in the normal course of nature is inconsistent with the judgement that God was the cause of it; and, indeed, goes so far as to accuse those who deny this of confusion or dishonesty.[35] God as Christians (or for that matter Muslims) have traditionally conceived him is not merely or chiefly that which accounts for otherwise inexplicable adaptation in the world. God is deemed to be that which *has made* all the things and *performs* all the events which now constitute the world, and *is changing* the world into the new kingdom of Christ; otherwise unaccountable order, if there be any, is only one aspect among others of the being and activity of this God.

The two views of belief in God which I have just summarized represent it as at least intelligible, if false as a matter of fact. In the last thirty years or so, it has been quite usual for philosophers to claim that belief in God does not even make sense. Radical empiricists claim that the only intelligible subjects of discourse are on the one hand what can be apprehended by the senses, and on the other hand the formal systems of logic and mathematics which depend on definition. Discourse about God conforms to neither of these requirements, and hence is held by radical empiricists to be nonsensical.[36] Now people sometimes treat the problem of how grounds within our experience can be the basis for belief in things and facts which are supposed to transcend our experience as though it were peculiar to theism and the more exuberant kinds of metaphysics.[37] But in fact the same problem turns up in areas of inquiry and speculation which it is far more implausible to dismiss as unintelligible. Other persons, for instance, transcend our experience of them in the sense that there is more to them (their thoughts and sensations) than could conceivably be directly experienced by us. But in fact we are in the habit of construing the thoughts and experiences of other persons by inference from their activities. *How* we make this inference is a question much disputed by philosophers, but *that* we make it is not usually doubted; and when this is denied, it is denied only at the cost of assertion of the implausible thesis that all statements about a man's thoughts and sensations are reducible without remainder to statements about his behaviour or the physical state of his brain.[38] Again, the facts of past history transcend any experiences by means of which present-day historians may come to know of them; for example, the proposition that Julius Caesar landed in Britain in 55 B.C. is not reducible without remainder to propositions asserting the grounds available to historians here and now for believing that he did so.[39] But if one accepts the intelligibility of statements about other minds and about the past, and admits at the same time that their meaning is not simply identical with propositions about the grounds which we can have for believing them, then it is hard consistently to exclude *a limine* the possibility that we may have insight into a being who himself transcends the world of our experience by inference from his activity within that world. It is difficult to see what empiricist principle would rule out such insight as logically impossible, which would not at the same time make insoluble the problems of other minds and of statements about the past.

Other arguments that the notion of "God" is conceptually confused do not depend on radical empiricism. The main theme of Professor A. G. N. Flew's *God and Philosophy* is the thesis that the concept of God is internally inconsistent, in the same sort of way that the notion of a square circle is. The following paragraphs will take the form of a kind of dialogue with Flew.

Flew argues that before we can take seriously what believers tell us about God and his revelation of himself to man, we have to be sure that the concept "God" is itself in order, and that the very use of the term does not commit us in some way to talking nonsense. So he examines the concept of God itself. He looks at the works of philosophers and theologians and lists the qualities which they have ascribed to God; God is supposed to be infinitely this and infinitely that; and Flew wonders how such attributes could be possessed severally, let alone together, by any individual. Flew asks the question *in abstracto*: How could all the qualities which people have ascribed to God belong to anything? I want to argue that this is not the right way to ask it. "God" is a term whose meaning was established, in an informal way, in the language of the Bible, long before philosophers and theologians started paying what Whitehead called "metaphysical compliments"[40] to this God. It was to the being so defined that the metaphysical compliments were offered, and it was by the fact that it was to this being that they were applied that the precise meanings of these terms, and the relation of these to their ordinary meanings, was established. The chapter on *God and Philosophy* which follows the introduction is called "Beginning from the Beginning". The chief contention underlying what I have to say is just that Flew has *not* begun from the beginning. To apply Flew's technique to modern nuclear physics would be to reason somewhat as follows: "Let us make sure that the concepts of an electron and a neutron are in order, before we take seriously what physicists have to tell us about electrons and neutrons." But of course it is virtually, if not completely, impossible to understand the concepts of neutron and electron apart from a certain amount of information about neutrons and electrons.

It is not enough, of course, just to state that Flew has started in the wrong place; it is necessary to show how, had he started from the right place, had he begun from what has been, as a matter of historical fact, the beginning, the outcome would have been different. As I have said, to judge from the Bible, "God", briefly, is that which makes the things and performs the events of which nature and history consist; and one learns to use the term "God" accordingly. The Israelites, when some national calamity occurred, ascribed it to the anger of this God, rather as someone might regard his own uncomfortable circumstances as due to the anger of one who had power over him; when they were delivered, they similarly ascribed this to God's mercy. J. O. Urmson has remarked that most general world-views construe reality in terms of a model derived from one small part of it;[41] this certainly seems to apply to the theistic world-view, which construes the world in terms of the actions of an intelligent agent.

It may rightly be objected that just to be willing to talk in these terms is not to believe in God. For the Christian theist, not only the mere possibility of talking in this way is at issue; he also believes that things *have* turned out and *will* turn out in such a way that this way of talking will be vindicated against its possible rivals. The Christian characteristically believes not only that things will turn out in such a way that the mourners will be comforted, the meek inherit the earth, and the merciful obtain mercy (cf. Matt. 5.3–10); but also that God has acted in a certain way in the past: that the man Jesus was born of a virgin, preached and performed miracles more or less as the New Testament writers claim that he did, was crucified and rose from the dead. Christian theism, in other words, goes with certain beliefs about matters of fact in the past (history) and the future (eschatology). It is not just a stance towards life, expressed in a certain form of language, though indeed it includes this; but it involves assent to certain propositions about matters of fact, such as render reasonable both the stance and the language that enshrines it. This aspect of Christian theism, its possession of truth-conditions which are putative matters of fact, makes it in some ways analogous to scientific theories, and prevents it from becoming merely a more or less moving or profound story, doing for experience as a whole what discourse about Santa Claus does for a small aspect of it.[42] Christian theists believe that God has shown his power in the past, and to some extent (in the experience they say they have of him within the fellowship of the Church) does so in the present; they therefore expect that he will be able to fulfil the promises which they allege he has made for the future. Since Christian theism in its traditional sense stands or falls with belief in particular matters of historical fact, it follows that it is as theoretically falsifiable as these putative matters of fact. I agree with Flew, against Bultmann and Tillich among many other influential contemporary theologians, that the objective truth or falsity of Christianity, as opposed to its mere profundity as a vision of life, depends on its theoretical vulnerability to certain kinds of rational inquiry.[43] If it were shown beyond reasonable doubt that the Gospels were wholly or largely false as a matter of historical fact—never mind their mythological or dramatic profundity as providing insight into human life, though of course they have this too—then Christian theism in its traditional sense would be proved false. But extreme scepticism as regards the historicity of the Gospels, however well it fits that fashion of theological subjectivism that plays into the hands of thinkers like Flew, can be contested on scientific grounds.[44]

The atheist does not characteristically believe that things have taken place as the Christian (or, for that matter, the Muslim, or the theistic Hindu) believes, or will turn out as the Christian expects; consequently, if he is at all disposed to use a term to stand as subject of active verbs whose objects are the things and events which constitute the world of our experience, he will not use the term "God", owing to its misleading associations.

Having prepared my ground at some length, I must return to what Flew alleges in detail. My general contention is that he has misunderstood language about God by not starting from the central paradigm cases of its use. He has looked at it "gone on holiday", and has then asked, rhetorically, "How could such language ever be at work?"—instead of actually looking at the language at work, which might have thrown light for him on why it looks as it does on holiday. I will take Flew's objections in order:[45]

(*a*) The fact that a word is used in discourse which is superficially intelligible does not prove that there is not some hidden contradiction latent in it (2.4—2.6). I have tried to show how theistic discourse *does* hang together, and also why it is that Flew thinks that it does not—briefly, that he has not considered the central and normal uses of the term "God", from which the senses of the more derivative uses which he does consider may most easily be understood. Flew cites the history of mathematics for examples of what he means; but it must be remembered that the term "God" does not only turn up in sophisticated theories, but is used in the language of ordinary people as well. One would have thought that any radical inconsistency involved in the use of a concept would be soon exposed by the wear and tear of ordinary usage. It is a suspicious fact that philosophers have frequently tried to make nonsense of other terms (for example "mind", "matter", and "time") which turn up frequently both in ordinary language and those more erudite and sophisticated segments of discourse which arise from reflection on it; the successors of these philosophers have generally held that they were mistaken.

(*b*) To make theological assertions invulnerable to claims about matters of fact, as has been done by some theologians, is to reduce them to insignificance (2.8). I have tried already to show, and will later do so at greater length, how, on the traditional interpretation, Christian theism is committed to certain assertions of fact, about the past and the future, which might well be disproved. That Christian theism must be theoretically falsifiable if it is to be true in anything like its traditional sense, I agree with Flew against (for example) Bultmann and Tillich among modern theologians.

(*c*) Central to Christian theism is the idea of a divine will which can be disobeyed, since the concepts of sin, of an atonement for sin, and of an incarnation of the deity which (at least on many understandings of the doctrine) is essentially a remedy for sin, depend on it. But it seems impossible to give sense to this idea of a divine will (2.9). The answer is that creation is supposed by the majority of Christians to be divided into inanimate beings, who cannot but do what God has ordained them to do, and rational beings, such as men and (it is usually believed) angels, who can disobey God if they will. This supposition of course involves the falsity of determinism, and of the view that the uncertainty of our forecasts of the future, in as far as this depends on human action, is a function merely of the incompleteness of our scientific knowledge. In other words, Christian theism, at least on the majority of traditional interpretations,[46] involves a human freedom more radical than the mere absence of constraint which it amounts to on the view of Hobbes, Hume, and many modern philosophers.[47] God's will for those creatures who can disobey him is identified partly by what contributes to the happiness and self-realization of creatures individually and collectively (natural law), and partly by special revelation in Scripture and the tradition of the Church, which is said both to support the said natural law as far as it goes and to supplement it.

(*d*) It is by no means clear how we can pick out God as an object of discourse (2.10). This problem is solved for the Christian by the fact that he learns how to use the term "God" through the language of Scripture and the Church, and so comes to understand that although all events take place by God's action, or at least (in the case of rebellious free agents) by his permission, some are his in the special sense that they stand out against the normal run of events as particularly expressive of his will for us. How this is so in detail must be left to the detailed discussion of the notions of grace, providence, and miracle.[48]

(*e*) Positive words of our language cannot characterize such a being as God is alleged to be; mere negations, as practised by exponents of the *via negativa*, are not to the point (2.10). What is needed, by way of positive identification, is some account of the way the term "God" should be used—what are to count as God's actions, God's commands, and so on. This I believe I have already provided in outline.

(*f*) The defining characteristics attributed to God seem inconsistent with each other and with known facts (2.10). I have suggested that most of the alleged incompatibilities disappear once you know what is being characterized, and consequently in what sense different from their usual one the characterizing descriptions are to be taken. The admitted fact of evil is incompatible with one understanding, certainly a very natural one, of the proposition "God is infinitely good". That this inconsistency makes the proposition itself glaringly false in as far as it is not totally meaningless is the most serious, in my opinion, of Flew's allegations.[49]

(*g*) The radically Christological solution, fashionable in some circles, to the problem of identifying God, will not work; since, asserting as it does that all statements about God can be replaced by statements about Jesus Christ, it makes "God" a redundant term (2.15). Here I agree with Flew; but I can afford to do so, since I think that God is independently characterizable in the way which I have described.

(*h*) Tillich's characterization of God as "being itself" is inadequate as identifying God with a mere abstraction. And the same really applies to Aquinas, who will have it that God is subsistent being itself, goodness itself, and truth itself (2.18—2.19). I think Flew's objection to this formula of Tillich's is justified; more satisfactory characterizations of God to be found in Tillich's work are "cause of being" and "ground of being", which approximate to the characterization which I suggested of God, as that short of whose existence and activity nothing else would exist or act. Flew's attempt to implicate Aquinas, as far as I can see, is mistaken.[50] That Aquinas does not accept that God is being itself, truth itself, and goodness itself, is quite the sense attributed to him by Flew, is clear from the terms in which he rejects certain suggestions of St Augustine—that if we admit truth to exist, and goodness to exist, we must admit God to exist, since God is truth and goodness. Aquinas in fact characterizes God first in terms of his relationship to the world, by means of the Five Ways; it is only subsequently that he tries to show that God is in some sense subsistent being, goodness, and truth, and in what sense he is so.[51]

I have suggested that the existence of God, while it is not a putative matter of fact in quite the same way as the existence of arthropods with mandibles is, does involve putative matters of empirical fact. One may distinguish usefully four concepts of God, each of which has a different bearing on possible human experience: (*a*) That which is said to make all the things and perform all the events of which nature and history consist; (*b*) the object of religious experience, or of veneration above all else; (*c*) that which will ultimately bring about a state of justice between rational agents; (*d*) that which brought it about that Jesus lived, died, and rose from the dead, more or less as the New Testament writers say that he did. To believe that God in sense (*a*) exists, it might be said, is little more than to be prepared to use a certain way of talking about the world. On the other hand, this is the God whose existence can most plausibly be said to be proved by philosophical argument; such argument can at least show the self-consistency of such a way of envisaging the world, which is perhaps a not inconsiderable virtue at a time when many philosophers believe that theism is internally incoherent. As to the connection of this God with the God Christians claim to have revealed himself in Christ—perhaps the best available statement of the matter is that of Father Herbert McCabe: that God in the former sense cannot be proved *not* to be God in the latter.[52] God in this sense is the operator who is not operand or transform, the First Cause of the world. That God exists in sense (*b*) is even more trivial and quite indisputable; there is no doubt that many people have experiences of the kind described as religious, or that they have "objects of ultimate concern" in that money, sexual delight, or revenge may be the supreme value giving directions to all their activities.[53] God's existence in sense (*c*) is by no means obvious or trivial. Since it is perfectly clear that justice is not done in the present life—that the good are often wretched and the wicked flourish—the existence of God in sense (*c*) entails an afterlife available to at least some men, either in an existence apart from the present world or by reincarnation within it. The work done by the concept of God in this sense is equivalent to that done by the Hindu and Buddhist concept of Karma, the principle which ensures that the agent can never ultimately evade the consequences of his wrong actions. If God exists in sense (*c*)—if the First Cause operates in nature, or apart from nature as we know it, in such a way that some kind of justice is ultimately done—one can see that the First Cause is a worthy object of worship, or at least a worthier one than if this were not so. The Christian characteristically believes in God in senses (*a*), (*b*), (*c*), and (*d*); the First Cause is worshipful in that, by incorporation into the community inaugurated by the mighty acts of Jesus Christ, man can ultimately come into a fellowship of bliss with him, and universal justice will come about. This is much as to say that Christians believe in God as Creator (him whose actions underlie the whole world order), as Redeemer (him who by his acts has delivered man, if man accepts the deliverance, from misery and the effects of his wrong action), and as Sanctifier (him who is preparing man for a future of unalloyed bliss and moral perfection).

The problem of whether the existence of God is subject to verification or falsification, and of the means by which it could be verified or falsified, will be different according to which of these four concepts of God, singly or in combination, is in question. The case against theism, that it is subject to no testing whatever in experience, has been set out very forcibly, as one might expect, by Flew.[54] That God exists, he argues, appears at first sight to be a good brash hypothesis, full of implications about how things will turn out. Now these implications do not seem to be fulfilled; but the theist, instead of abandoning his hypothesis, successively qualifies it until its *prima facie* meaning is reduced to nothing. (The effect of this is rather as though someone stated that water consisted of a compound of helium and argon, though he readily admitted the validity of all the experiments which have led to and confirmed the belief that water is a compound of hydrogen and oxygen.) God is our Father and loves us, the theist says. The example is raised against him of a child dying of cancer of the throat, whose loving human father, though desperate to help, can do nothing. Apparently his alleged heavenly father, though *ex hypothesi* he *can* do anything, in fact does nothing. The theist replies that divine love is something very different from human love, so different that God, unlike human lovers, will take no step to save his beloved from atrocious agony, though perfectly capable of doing so. But once this qualification has been made, as it must be in face of all the horrifying facts of human misery, what sense remains in saying that there is a loving God at all? How would things be different, according to the theist, if God did not exist, or if he hated rather than loved us?

The same point may be made in relation to other propositions apparently implied by the theistic hypothesis. That the world is created by God once seemed to imply that it had come into being at some time in the past; and also that it showed an adaptation of means to ends otherwise inexplicable than by the contrivance of an intelligent agent. Nowadays theists seem inclined to deny these *prima facie* implications of their position, owing to the pressure of modern science, while still insisting, in spite of this, that the world is created by God.

A similar point has been made by W. W. Bartley, who in his book *The Retreat to Commitment* applies to Christian theism the moral of the philosophical theories of Karl Popper. According to Popper, a theory is vindicated as representing the truth about the world to the degree that, although experience *might* have falsified it, in fact it *does* not do so. In deciding between two theories, the thing to do is to look for experimental evidence which *falsifies* one of them; there is no difficulty in finding *some* evidence to *verify* any theory whatever. Popper's theories were originally worked out as a critique of science; but their application to religion is not far to seek. Now Christian theism, which once appeared to be a candidate for truth in that scientific discovery, say in the sphere of historical fact, might have falsified it, is now represented by prominent exponents (Bartley cites Barth and Tillich) as such that no experience is relevant to deciding its truth or falsity. But it has purchased its invulnerability to scientific inquiry only at the high cost of its claim to represent the truth about the world.

There are two possible ways out of this difficulty for the theist; he can either say that he is under no obligation to meet the demand, or he can show that he can in fact meet it. It seems to me that the demand *is* a valid one, in that, if theism does not meet it, it tends to be indistinguishable from a mere subjective picture of reality, available for and useful to some, but with no real claim to be true. But I shall argue that, whether the demand is a valid one or not, traditional Christian theism can meet it. God's existence, as I have said, is evidently subject to verification or falsification to different degrees according to which of the senses outlined earlier it is understood in. If the existence of God is understood in sense (*a*), its assertion amounts to little more than assertion of the availability of a way of talking; if in sense (*b*), it is indubitably true, since there is unquestionably such a thing as "religious experience", but it is trivial. But if understood in senses (*a*), (*b*), (*c*), and (*d*), the existence of God entails something about the past, something about the present, and something about the future. The relation between the three is finely set out in the following passage by Ian Crombie, which has the merit of showing both *what* it is to believe in traditional Christianity, and *why* some people believe it.

. . . we cannot believe that God loves us, if that is supposed to be in any sense a statement of sober fact. . . . The Christian does not attempt to evade it (the objection) either by helter-skelter flight, or by impudent bluff. He has his prepared positions onto which he retreats; and he knows that if these positions are taken, then he must surrender. He does not believe that they can be taken, but that is another matter. There are three main fortresses behind which he goes. For, *first*, he looks for the resurrection of the dead, and the life of the world to come; he believes, that is, that we do not see all of the picture, and that the parts which we do not see are precisely the parts which determine the design of the whole. He admits that if this hope be vain then we are of all men the most miserable. *Second*, he claims that he sees in Christ the verification, and to some extent also the specification, of the divine love. That is to say, he finds in Christ not only convincing evidence of God's concern for us, but also what sort of love the divine love is, what sort of benefits God is concerned to give us. He sees that, on the New Testament scale of values, it is better for a man to lose the whole world if he can thereby save his soul (which means his relationship to God); and that for that hope it is reasonable to sacrifice all that he has, and to undergo the death of the body and the mortification of the spirit. *Third*, he claims that in the religious life, of others, if not as yet in his own, the divine love may be encountered, that the promise "I will not fail thee nor forsake thee" is, if rightly understood, confirmed there. If, of course, this promise is interpreted as involving immunity from bodily suffering, it will be refuted; but no reader of the New Testament has any right so to interpret it. It is less glaringly, but as decisively, wrong to interpret it as involving immunity from spiritual suffering; for in the New Testament only the undergoing of death (which means the abdication of control over one's destiny) can be the beginning of life.[55]

The historical truth-conditions of traditional Christianity have in common with other putative historical facts, and also with those investigated by such a science as palaeontology or any other kind of inquiry concerned with the past, that they are not subject to such conclusive testing here and now as are, say, the typical propositions of physics or chemistry. On the other hand, what we may discover here and now may make their truth more or less probable. It is characteristic of all statements about the past that, while they are not subject to such conclusive corroboration or refutation as are some statements concerning the present or the future, evidence may accumulate in such a way as to make it more rational, or less rational, to believe them. If an unbiased examination of the New Testament documents, which took into account the probable lapse of time between their origin and the occurrence of the events which they describe, were to make it plausible to suppose that Jesus never existed, or was a wholly different kind of person from what is claimed, then it would be correspondingly irrational to be a Christian in the traditional sense of the word. In the present circumstances of his life, the Christian thinks that he experiences and observes the power of God, hurting and wounding but also giving help and comfort; also, especially when worshipping in the company of other believers, he has moments of intense bliss which he interprets as an anticipation of the promised future life in the presence of God. For this consummation he can only wait and hope. To put it briefly: owing to his belief in God's mighty acts in the *past*, and experience of his sanctifying power in the *present*, Christians believe he will fulfil his promises in the *future*. That what is alleged, for instance, in the Apostles' Creed *has* happened, *is* happening, and *will* happen, is what it is for traditional Christian theism to represent the truth about the world.

The analysis of belief in God here proposed certainly will not be agreed to universally; the fact is that many who call themselves Christians and claim to believe in God do not have the beliefs which on this account they should have. Not the least of the difficulties lying in the way of understanding the meaning of belief in God is the fact that theologians and philosophers of religion themselves present accounts of their belief which are not only divergent, but actually mutually inconsistent. One authority will say, in line with my own suggestions, that the truth of religious belief involves that events in the world will turn out in a certain way; another will counter that not only does religious belief not involve this, but to claim that it does is to show that one has radically misunderstood its nature. The difficulty has been well expressed by D. Z. Phillips:

Philosophers who say they believe in God give widely different accounts of their beliefs. Some of them say that to believe in God is to believe in an ultimate order of fact; that ultimately a certain state of affairs is going to be the case. To trust in God is to trust that this state of affairs will come about. The truth or falsity of religion is determined by whether or not this ultimate hope, this eschatological expectation, is to be realized or not. Other philosophers deny that this account has anything to do with religion, and hold that in fact it blinds one to its true nature. To say that religious faith is an expectation of certain states of affairs being the case is to confuse it with idolatry. The strength of religion is in its independence of the way things go.[56]

Before the philosopher of religion tries to adjudicate between the rival accounts, he should try to achieve a viewpoint from which they can both be understood. As a matter of fact, in the case of historical Christianity and to a large extent the other religions as well, the fundamental structure of religious belief can be presented roughly as follows: (*a*) In the context of certain beliefs about the future of man, founded upon promises alleged to have been given in the past, (*b*) an experience of present mastery over worldly pleasures and sufferings becomes possible, and (*c*) moral policies seem worthwhile which otherwise would not have been so. So are related what one might label the factual, the mystical, and the moral elements of traditional religion; in the case of Christianity, the existence of each of these elements, and the relationship between them, can be shown throughout the New Testament. To give only a few examples: St Paul calls the present experience of life in the spirit a foretaste and guarantee of what is to come (thus relating element *b* to *a*), and says that apart from expectation of a future life, Christians, to judge from their present activities and experiences, would be the most wretched of men (relating *b* and *c* to *a*). The Beatitudes of Jesus, and his parables counselling watchfulness, also bring out the connection between elements *c* and *a*.[57]

It has often been argued that, if the nature of Christian faith is properly understood, it will be seen that the results of historical inquiry are irrelevant to it. In his *Philosophical Fragments*, Kierkegaard makes a thoroughgoing distinction between the *fact* of God's incarnation in Christ and the historical *sign* of this. God's sign of his presence in history is bound to be grudging, he says, just in case a man should be so foolish as to confuse the sign with what it signifies. The historical sign *as* historical, in abstraction from its role as signifying God's presence, is of no importance at all; whether it is a matter of the mighty works which Jesus performed, or of the impressive words which he uttered. To marvel at these words and works for themselves is totally to miss the point; what is at stake is not that a remarkable human individual lived at the stated time, but a summons to faith in the God who was revealed to him. It follows that some contemporary observer who kept the most careful possible note of everything that Jesus said and did would not be any the closer to being a true disciple of his. If this is the case, it may be seen that the contemporary of Jesus is in no better position to have faith in the God revealed in him than the man who succeeds him in time by eighteen hundred years or more. To be sure, the contemporary can go and look. But only the sign of God's presence will be visible; God will not be visible as such. Talk about being impressed by the bearing of Jesus, or by what he said, is all silly twaddle; this is all talk about the sign, not about the presence of God itself, which is the only important thing. Either the man who encounters the sign itself, or who hears about it at second hand, acknowledges in faith what is signified, or he does not do so; the most subtle human reasoning is of no avail in the matter. The attempt to prove that faith is rational is a total waste of time, since the God of whose presence the historical Jesus is a sign wholly transcends human reason. Even the accuracy of the historical sources about Jesus is by no means of over-riding importance—here indeed is a province within which human reasoning might have something worth declaring—since these again have a bearing only on the sign, and no bearing on the only matter which is of fundamental importance, that in this sign the presence of God is revealed. If the generation contemporary with Jesus had passed on to their successors nothing more than that God had come among them in the form of a humble man, that he walked and talked with them, and at length died, that would be enough and more than enough for faith.[58]

This argument has had a powerful influence on recent theology. It is central to the whole theological endeavour of Bultmann, for instance, that no inquiry into the facts about the historical Jesus can have any bearing on his status as the bearer of the Word of God.[59] Yet the argument as it stands is fallacious; and it is questionable how far its proponents are willing to take it to its logical conclusion. Is it not possible that historical inquiry might provide very good reasons for asserting that Jesus never existed, or that he was an unscrupulous trickster with political ambitions? Admittedly, as Kierkegaard rightly insists, there is a great deal *more* to Christian belief than that the historical Jesus was not radically dissimilar from how the Gospels represent him; but this may well be acknowledged, while it may still be insisted that it is *at least* this. If the alleged sign of God's presence were a wicked man, or if he never existed at all, this surely would constitute good *prima facie* grounds for denying that God did reveal himself through him. It is sometimes argued, again, that historical inquiry is by its very nature doomed to uncertainty in its conclusions, and hence can never aspire to the status of an objective science; the man of faith has thus a certainty about the person of Jesus that no historical argument can shake. But this is to neglect the fact that historical inquiry may at least *approach* certainty in its conclusions. History differs in method from, say, physics; but the fundamental principle that hypotheses are propounded, and then tested against the available evidence, is the same in both forms of inquiry. Some historical hypotheses are incompatible with Christianity; but, for all we know for certain, it might be just these hypotheses which are progressively confirmed as more and more light is thrown on the relevant place and period. The man of faith believes that this will not *in fact* be so; but, at the risk of evacuating his beliefs of much of their meaning as traditionally understood, he must believe that it might conceivably be so.

What applies to history applies also to other areas of human knowledge and opinion in relation to faith. Metaphysical materialism and phenomenalism are evidently inconsistent with Christian theism (since God is neither a material object nor a bundle of perceptions) in a way that, say, the Cartesian and Aristotelian philosophies are not; to that extent, good arguments which corroborated materialism or phenomenalism would also tell against Christian theism. The same applies to mortality. It is not a matter of finding historical, moral, or metaphysical *proofs* of faith; it is rather a matter of establishing whether faith is of a piece with the beliefs on these matters which we have come to on other grounds, or whether it makes nonsense of them and is made nonsense of by them. The dilemma that the option for or against faith must be either capable of rational proof, or not amenable to rational consideration at all, is a false one.[60] For example, we build up our moral opinions on the basis of our experience of life in general, and the opinions of others whom we deem worthy of trust. If the moral attitudes which are of a piece with Christian theism went clean against these, or if they were shown in general to have destructive rather than beneficial effects on individual and social life, then this would constitute good rational grounds for rejecting Christian theism.

To deny that particular beliefs about the past and the future have in fact characterized the Christian faith from New Testament times onwards would be absurd. However, religious language is often used to foster and express either the feeling of mystical transcendence of mundane difficulties, *or* Christian moral policies, *or* both, quite apart from the beliefs about matters of fact with which these have traditionally been associated, or even in such a way that to have the expectations or to set any store by them seems inconsistent with "true religion". But the fact is that to set store by such expectations of the future has characterized the religion of the vast majority of religious people. It may well be that a more refined religious feeling, or advances in our knowledge of the world, may make it proper for us to understand belief in God in a manner radically different from the traditional one. But if this is so, it is of the first importance for us to understand clearly what is involved; and that we should not use expressions like "true religion" to insinuate that what is being commended is more similar to what has usually been known as "religion" up to now than would appear from an impartial examination of the facts of the case. At least it is vital to *describe* adequately the nature and function of religion and belief in God as they have been up to now before one tries to *revise* them.

In this chapter I have tried to set out clearly how God's activity is supposed by traditional Christian theists, and *mutatis mutandis* by theists of other kinds, to be related to the things and events which constitute the world of our experience. I have tried to contrast this traditional conception of God with more limited views of his alleged nature and function which are prevalent, and to prove that attempts to show that theism is logically incoherent are ill-judged. It remains to relate the fundamental view of God and his dealings with the world here outlined to the dependent concepts of grace, evil, prayer, providence, and miracle.

2 GRACE

According to the teaching of the New Testament and of the traditional Christian Church as a whole, man has become alienated from God through his own fault, and the result has been suffering and disharmony in the individual, in society, and in man's relation to the physical world. But God has acted on man's behalf, offering him renewed fellowship with himself and the healing of his wounded nature. This renovation of human nature, which the Church exists to proclaim and prefigure, is as yet incomplete and only to be fully realized in future. The help which God offers to man to overcome the results of his sin and to bring him to eternal life is what is called the "grace" of God.

The New Testament presents man as, in effect, going through three states, in which he is successively under the dominion of sin, in a state of grace, and fully redeemed. When referring to man in his state of sin and alienation from God, St Paul talks of him as "in Adam" and "in the flesh", St John as conformed to "the world".[1] In this state the written law for Jews, and natural conscience for Gentiles, make men conscious of their sin, which however they are powerless to overcome.[2] Since the impulses of God's grace go against the concerns and desires of sinful and alienated man, it is bound to appear as "wrath".[3]

But once incorporated into the new society "in Christ", man is "a new creation", subject as such to a new law.[4] This new form of life is characterized by a new pattern of behaviour, by love, joy, and peace—what St Paul calls "fruits of the Spirit";[5] but also by a tussle of the old and new principles for mastery.[6] This is graphically presented in the exorcisms and healings of the Gospels, in which Christ fights Satan, the evil one who has power over the world, on man's behalf.[7] St John's Gospel develops a whole series of analogies for the way in which man is dependent on Christ for this new life—Christ is the light without which his people are in darkness, the shepherd without which they stray, the bread without which they starve, the life without which they die.

But this state of fellowship with God here and now available to man on earth is only an anticipatory pledge of the life to come.[8] In a manner, the new community already sits with Christ in the heavenly places; but the quality of its present life depends on joyful anticipation of the future.[9] If this were not so, Christians would be of all men the most miserable.[10] To show the life of the Kingdom of God here and now—to be merciful, to love peace, to feed the hungry, and to clothe the naked—is to be bound for eternal life with Christ. On the other hand, to remain in the old form of life, self-closed to God's offered grace, is to forfeit eternal life.[11]

There are certainly difficulties and obscurities in the New Testament view of the state of man in relation to God; but the main outlines are clear enough. Man, by reason of his own fault turned away from God and consequently warped in his own nature, has been brought into a relationship with God such that he is able, always with God's help, to come to eternal life. This relationship with God issues both in a new kind of life here and now, and in bliss hereafter. There has been a tendency among some modern Protestant writers, among whom Bultmann and Tillich are perhaps the more notable, to see the operation of God's grace in human life only in the here-and-now and with no reference to the consummation hereafter. But this is a serious distortion of the New Testament picture. There has been a salutary corrective in the work of some very recent theologians,[12] who have portrayed the promised Kingdom of God in terms not so much of authentic existence available for the individual here and now, as of a just and happy social order towards which men ought to devote their efforts. Fr Herbert McCabe has actually described the Church as "the sacrament of the socialist society". But what applies to the understanding of the promises of God in terms of the philosophy of Heidegger applies also to the understanding of them in terms of the philosophy of Marx; the Kingdom of God as Christians await it may include authentic existence for the individual and the end of class-structures for society, but amounts to more than either or both of them. It is essential to the Kingdom of God as Christians understand it that some at least of those who have died will have a real share in it; and surely no secular vision of the future could expect the resurrection of the dead without ceasing to be such.

But once this limitation is accepted, it is clear that any account of human individuals and society which contrasts the wickedness and misery of them as they actually are with the virtue and happiness which might be theirs can be used to illustrate and make intelligible the contrast made by Christian doctrine between man in a state of sin and man redeemed. As Tillich says, "man experiences his present situation in terms of disruption, conflict, self-destruction, meaninglessness, and despair in all realms of life"; he thus hopes for "a reality in which the self-estrangement of our existence is overcome, a reality of reconciliation and reunion, of creativity, meaning, and hope".[13] According to Christian belief, God will surely bring such a state of affairs to pass, and all who accept the operation of God's grace on them here and now will have a share in it. As Aquinas says, grace does not take away nature, but perfects it; and as a natural consequence adds to nature what nature sees to be lacking in itself. This is just what one might expect to ensue from the doctrine that it is one God who creates and redeems. As Karl Rahner has put it, "the closest proximity of the world to God is also its most complete liberation to be itself".[14]

It is perhaps a specially modern insight, deriving particularly from the work of Freud and Marx and their disciples, that there may be moral poison in a social or economic system as such, and not simply in the individuals who comprise it. Our "original sin" may be regarded as our membership from the very first of these corrupt forms of society, out of which we ought to opt for membership of the good society which God is bringing into existence, and of which the Church is the anticipatory symbol. The question of what the relationship is between being in a state of grace and being a member of the Church is a crucial one for theology. Considering the number of Christians who by their own Christian lights are bad men, and the number of non-Christian or anti-Christians who by the same lights are comparatively good men, it would evidently be absurd to say that only members of the Christian Church are in a state of grace. Rahner has suggested very reasonably that men of goodwill, who follow their conscience where it leads them and do the good as they see it, are in a state of grace and so in an inchoate way members of the Church.[15] If God wills all men to be saved (and many have never heard the Gospel, and some of those who have know it only as presented through words or lives which outrage their moral sensibilities), Rahner's opinion seems to be an all but necessary conclusion.

There are a number of philosophical problems connected with the doctrine of grace which have troubled Hindu and Islamic as well as Christian theists. The essence of the doctrine is that God acts upon man in such a way as to save him from his sin and the consequences of it; and the query naturally arises how God's action is related to man's co-operation in the matter.

Through the operation of grace God restores the relationship between himself and man which has been broken by man's rebellion, and in so doing repairs the defects in society and individual men. From biblical times until the end of the last century, moral evil was regarded as being a largely individual affair, however widespread the suffering that resulted; the manner in which social institutions can make "sinful" behaviour by individuals virtually inevitable was not appreciated. The truth has been brought home to twentieth-century intellectuals by Marx and Freud in their very different ways, but has perhaps been expressed most unforgettably in the novels of Dickens, particularly those of his late period. A society is bad so far as its institutions are such as to frustrate individual liberty and development and to set its members the dilemma of either submitting by immolation of themselves or resorting to totally destructive rebellion. In a bad society institutional and individual moral evil reinforce one another; and men are punished, in society at large and in the intimate society of the family, by authority, for becoming and doing what the same authority has made it almost if not entirely inevitable that they should become and do. The Christian theist and the secularist of goodwill share the same hope of, and work for, a state of society in which these mutually reinforcing evils may be minimized. For the secularist, hope for such a society may be and perhaps must ultimately be forlorn; but the Christian theist is confident that, if not through man's efforts, then in spite of them, a just and happy society will ultimately be brought into being by God.

The Church exists to proclaim and prefigure, and to make its members fit for, this state of affairs which God has promised. Like other societies, the Church has her rites of initiation, renewal and recovery, which are deemed to be means by which God helps the individual believer; these rites are what are known as the sacraments. It is a maxim of Catholic sacramental theology that the sacraments "cause by signifying"[16] the operation of God's grace on men. Just as the sentence "I hate you" may both signify one man's hatred of another and implement it by making the latter unhappy for a week, so the sacraments, the effective expression of

God's love for his children, are deemed by Christian theists both to signify the promoting and renewing of their life with God and to bring it about, the latter by means of the former. The sacraments are distinguishable from magic just because it is by way of their meaning, and not as it were physically or chemically, that the life of the Christian with God is fostered. That they act in such a way is a consequence of the belief that God acts on rational creatures while respecting their free will, and not, at least typically, by over-riding it. To influence another by words or signs is to respect his freedom, in a way that merely to work upon him physically or chemically, say by physical contraint or the injection of hormones, does not. By baptism the new life of the Christian is inaugurated, by confirmation he takes its full responsibilities on himself, by communion he is nourished and sustained in it, and by penance he is restored from defections from it.

Grace is a special instance of the operation of God upon his creatures. In as far as God is properly said to be active in every event which happens, the actions of free creatures are themselves actions of God; but in order to make sense of the concept of grace, one has to distinguish between those actions which are in some sense the creature's own and those influences which, by impinging on the creature from outside, enable it to act, if only by fostering its latent abilities. Aquinas says that God acts on his creatures in accordance with the nature of each;[17] in the cybernetic jargon which I introduced earlier, one might put it that each type of operand is subject to that kind of transformation which is appropriate to itself.

It is necessary, in order to get an adequate view of what Christians mean by grace, to view it in its full context. It is that whole operation by which God brings man to the final end for which he has created him—that is to say, bliss in a reconstituted world. Within this operation it is useful to distinguish, in the first place, between the original setting of the scenes so that a man will be put in the way of salvation, the helping of the man when he is consciously acting under the influence of grace, and the ultimate bringing of him to beatitude. (Roman Catholic theologians in the period after the Reformation labelled these three sorts of divine activity respectively prevenient, co-operating, and efficacious grace.) Since a man is who and what he is only in relation to the social groups of which he is a member, the bringing of man to beatitude will typically, though presumably not invariably,[18] involve his incorporation into the community whose *raison d'être* is the bringing of individuals and mankind at large to beatitude. This community, according to Christians, is the Church. On this view of grace, the "religious experience" which may be one of the results of God's operation upon us here and now is not significant only or chiefly for itself, but rather as an anticipation of the beatitude towards which we are being brought.

Grace is a kind of influence which one being can exercise upon another, and it may be compared and contrasted with other kinds of influence. Evidently, in the kinds of influence which we as agents can exert upon other things, there is a continuum from the crudest to the most subtle kinds. There is a gradation from pushing a block of wood along a floor, through making a plant grow more quickly by adding fertilizer to the soil, through inducing a horse to drink, to making a man change the course of his action by telling him that his dinner is ready. A man cannot merely be physically and chemically manipulated (like the block of wood or the plant); he can also be led (like the horse); and not only manipulated and led, but also rationally persuaded. The operation of divine grace seems to me typically to combine all three forms of influence; when it goes against or has no bearing on a man's will, it is analogous to physical or chemical manipulation, whereas, when it assists and fosters it, it is analogous to leading or rational persuasion. Teilhard de Chardin talked of the "divinization" of our "activities" and our "passivities";[19] by this he means, I think, that God acts upon us for our ultimate good both in what happens to us against our will and in what he enables us to do willingly in obedience to him.

Our common ideas of what it is to be persuaded or led seem to depend on the assumption—which some have held to be a misapprehension—that the being who is persuaded or led could have refused to be so. Different views on the nature of grace will follow according to whether one believes this assumption to be true or not. According to the thesis that I shall call determinist, our conviction that a man can do other than in fact he does is only a function of the incompleteness of our knowledge. On the contrary libertarian thesis, it is characteristic of at least some human actions that, however much were known by an observer of the antecedent circumstances, he could not know for certain which particular one of a range of actions would be performed. That we are free in the sense that we are not always subject to external constraint is not, of course, denied by determinists. They agree that many human acts are free in that the agent acts according to his wishes and intentions without these being subject to interference of a physical or neurotic nature. Hobbes compares the case of a river, which is said to flow freely in as far as its course is unobstructed; no one would be likely to infer from this that the freely-flowing water did not move according to determinate laws, and in such a way as could be predicted, if one knew the initial conditions and the relevant laws, with complete success. Similarly, it is argued, human beings are free in as far as they pursue their aims without interference; but that they have these aims, and act to realize them exactly as they do, could be infallibly forecast by anyone who had complete knowledge of them and of the forces acting upon them up to the time of such action.[20]

If this kind of freedom is the only kind that human agents possess, and if they do not have that more radical kind of freedom which implies that the proposition "He could have acted differently" is sometimes true of any being said to be free, certain important consequences follow for our conception of divine grace. If human beings are so constituted that they cannot do otherwise than they do, and if every man is bound for an eternity of bliss or misery, it follows that God as prime operator acts in such a way that any man who reaches bliss cannot do otherwise; and the same applies to any who may fail to reach it. Given the existence of heaven and hell as bliss or misery (or at least the absence of bliss) in the afterlife, and given that it is the destiny of every man to end up either in heaven or in hell, one of three consequences inevitably follows. Either God creates all men so that they cannot do other than go to hell, or he creates all men such that they cannot do other than go to heaven, or he creates some such that they cannot do other than go to heaven and others such that they cannot do other than go to hell. No Christian theologian has accepted the first possibility. The second (universalism) was accepted by Origen and commends itself to a large number of contemporary theologians. The third way out was taken by Calvin and his followers of the Reformed Churches. But the great majority of Christian theologians attribute to men at least enough freedom, in the radical sense, to accept or reject the grace which God offers them; and conclude that, if any man goes to hell, it is through his own fault.

Calvin frankly accepts the full conclusions which follow from his position. God does not send the wicked to hell, he says, because of their bad actions, but causes them to do bad actions because he is sending them to hell. We cannot say that God is unjust in doing this, since there is no standard of justice to which God is morally obliged to conform, justice being dependent on the divine will, which is itself subject to nothing. There is no reason why God should not have created everyone for the scrap-heap, and the wonder is not why all are *not* brought to bliss, but why any *are* so. To the question of how God can blame any man for disobeying his commandments, when he has actually foreordained him to do so, Calvin answers that a distinction must be made between God's real will, according to which everything happens that does happen, and his revealed command, which puts wicked men in the wrong and justifies their ultimate consignment to hell.[21] Calvin's position is usually objected to on the obvious, but perhaps none the less compelling, ground, that it is inconsistent with the goodness and mercifulness generally attributed to God. Also it goes clean contrary to the plain meaning of one New Testament text, to the effect that God wills all men to be saved.[22] Far more commonly held at the present time is the universalist theory, that God will ultimately bring all men to heaven. The difficulty with universalism, as far as the conscientious Christian theologian is concerned, is simply that it is not at all easy to square with a great deal of the teaching of the New Testament, which very often mentions hell, and the forfeiting by a man of the bliss which God has graciously offered him, as a real possibility.

To assert determinism, then, is to go against the vast majority of Christian theologians, and seems to have as its inevitable consequence the denial of tenets which are fairly central to Christian theism as a whole. But it may be felt on scientific or philosophical grounds that determinism is certainly true. The difficulties latent in the contradictory view are excellently summarized by Roderick Chisholm.[23] Chisholm says that if we wish to assert that we are responsible for any of our choices (which most of us, determinists included, do wish to assert), we must deny at least one of the following propositions: (*a*) that if we could not have avoided making a choice in the way we did, then we are not responsible for making that choice in the way we did; (*b*) that if we make a choice under conditions which render it causally impossible that the choice should have been made otherwise than it was, then we could not have avoided making that choice as we did; (*c*) that our choices are all made under conditions which render it causally impossible for them not to be made as they are made; (*d*) that "the making of a choice is the occurrence of an event". (What is meant by this curious assertion will appear in due course.)

Chisholm says (in this paragraph I shall expound his argument without comment) that (*a*) is a logical truth; in other words, that "I was morally responsible for this choice" strictly entails "I could have avoided making it as I did". Someone might deny (*b*) on the grounds that, when we say that an agent could have avoided making a choice as he did, we need mean only that he would have avoided doing so had he reflected further. But this manoeuvre seems rather to displace the problem than to resolve it; since it is surely right to counter that if the agent could not have avoided not reflecting further, and if the choice in question and its issue followed with causal necessity from this failure, then the agent could not have avoided making this choice as he did. Suppose, then, that we deny (*c*), making the claim that some of our choices just do not have causal preconditions such that we could not have avoided making them as we do. But this seems to imply that they are merely a matter of chance, which consorts no better with our responsibility for them than does their being causally predetermined. "We seem confronted . . . with a dilemma: either our choices have sufficient causal conditions or they do not; if they do have sufficient causal conditions they are not avoidable; if they do not they are fortuitous or capricious; and therefore, since our choices are either unavoidable or fortuitous, we are not morally responsible for them.[24] To deny (*d*) is to leave oneself free to assert that, while all *events* are causally determined, *choices* are not. Kant's well-known demand that for moral reasons we should regard agents as free, though acknowledging causal determinism in those events which constitute the world as examined by empirical science, is an attempt to avoid the conclusion by, in effect, denying proposition (*d*). But this denial seems suspiciously *ad hoc*, a desperate effort to avoid the conclusion that we are not responsible for any of our choices, when all other avenues of escape seem to have been blocked.

I agree completely with Chisholm's comments on (*a*) and (*b*), and, with rather more reservations, with those he makes on (*d*). The solution for the libertarian, it seems to me, is to deny that there are compelling, or even highly plausible, reasons for accepting (*c*). Chisholm, following Hume and many others, seems to accept the view that all events which are not predetermined are arbitrary. But an event or an action may be arbitrary in at least two senses:

(*a*) that it occurs in accordance with no plan or intelligible course of action on the part of its agent;

(*b*) that it could not have been predicted with certainty on the basis of knowledge, however complete, of what preceded it.

Now it seems to me that the libertarian thesis is quite coherent if taken to mean that rational free choices are arbitrary in the second sense, but not in the first. "But if we know what the agent's plan is, we know what he will do in accordance with it." But sometimes a person, for some reason or other, doesn't act according to plan. "Then, if we know what these reasons are, we will know both *that* he will deviate from his plan, and *how* he will do so." But this is just what the question is. The libertarian will argue that the person in this case is free to go on acting according to his original plan, or to deviate from it. "But since deviations from his plan are *ipso facto* arbitrary, he cannot be held responsible for them." This by no means follows. An action may be arbitrary in relation to one plan of action, but not so in relation to another. There is no need to assume that one who knows what a man's duties are, and what his inclinations are, and what other influences impinge upon him, will be able to infer that he will change his general intention or, if so, exactly when or how he will do so. Suppose, in a case of conflict between a man's inclination and what he believes to be his duty, the man at length follows his inclination. That he does so is quite comprehensible; but if he had not done so, his action in performing his duty and resisting his inclination would have been equally comprehensible. Just because he follows one comprehensible course of action rather than another, it by no means follows that an observer in possession of all the relevant facts would be able to judge it impossible that he should have acted in any way differently from the manner in which he did in fact act. From the intelligibility of one course of action, even when all the relevant circumstances are taken into account, the absolute arbitrariness of any alternative by no means follows, unless the thesis of determinism be assumed from the start.[25]

It has been argued, for example by Hume, that we do not allow that an agent is responsible for any action of his which is not determined by his character.[26] But it seems to me that, on the contrary, it is just when we wish to say that, given the kind of person the agent is, he could not have done otherwise than he did, that we *deny* his responsibility. The difference between a thief who is a kleptomaniac and a thief who is not is that the kleptomaniac cannot do other than steal, given the kind of person he is and the situation in which he finds himself; whereas the thief who is not a kleptomaniac is such that while he steals, and while to steal is *consistent* with the kind of person that he is, it is not absolutely *necessary* for him to do so. It is possible, of course, that there is in fact no thief who is not also a kleptomaniac (on the above definition), as indeed must be the case if determinism is true; but this is very far from being proved. Hume's claim gains what plausibility it has (and it has certainly convinced many recent philosophers) from the fact that, if we deem an action to be wholly inconsistent with an agent's character, we doubt if he is really responsible for it. But the claim that an action is *consistent* with its agent's character is a great deal weaker than the claim that it is *determined* by it. In a particular situation several courses of action may be consistent with a person's character; and there is no compelling reason to affirm that, if our knowledge of the agent's character were complete, we would know that he cannot but perform the action which he does in fact perform. On the libertarian account of the matter, we make our character as we go along; what we cannot help being owing to our heredity and the things which have happened to us which are outside our control, and what we have made ourselves to be by the free actions which constitute our previous history, while they strongly influence our present action, do not wholly determine it. And as I have already argued, to say that an action is not determined is by no means to say that it is random or wholly inexplicable.[27] It is sometimes said that the question of whether all events are physically predetermined, and the question of whether human acts are free, are irrelevant to one another. On the account which I am giving here, indeterminacy is a necessary but not a sufficient condition of radical freedom.

"But the more human action is studied by psychologists and

sociologists, the more we find that actions which appeared to us to be free are not so." Certainly, to make advances in, say, criminology, is to discover how certain hereditary patterns or environmental situations predispose individuals to commit certain types of crime. That a certain type of crime is committed by a certain type of person seems no longer arbitrary, but comprehensible. In as far as criminology advances, it renders crimes comprehensible which once seemed arbitrary; but I have already adduced reasons for doubting whether to render a human action comprehensible by one's explanation is *eo ipso* to show that it was necessitated. And even so far as sociological investigation does in fact restrict the alleged sphere of free action, as opposed to that of merely arbitrary action, it only implies that the sphere of free actions is narrower than one might suppose, and does not seem in a fair way to reducing it to vanishing-point. However many times an angle is bisected, an infinite number of straight lines can be drawn through each resultant angle. Because psychological and sociological studies restrict the supposed range of human freedom, there is no adequate reason to suppose that they will ultimately eliminate it altogether. It is sometimes said that to accept an explanation of human actions in terms such as those of psychoanalysis is implicitly to accept determinism. I believe that this is a mistake, though why it is so I can only indicate briefly. A man who accepts a psychoanalytic explanation of his own behaviour sees it as an intelligible series of strategies, all of them *comprehensible* but not thereby causally *necessary*, in relation to his environment, in order to come to terms with it; this enables him to avoid either self-pity (which is a consequence of minimizing one's responsibility) or self-castigation (which comes from exaggerating one's independence of circumstances). To recover from neurosis is precisely to accept a reasonable responsibility for one's situation. And if Chisholm and common sense are right, that to be responsible for one's action is to be able to act otherwise than one actually does, and if the brief characterization I have given of psychoanalysis is at all correct, there are grounds for holding not only that psychoanalysis does not presuppose determinism, but that it presupposes libertarianism.

The fact, which social science presupposes, that reliable predictions may be obtained of the behaviour of large masses of people, does not prove that such reliable predictions might be obtained of every individual constituting these masses, any more than the determinism (for practical purposes) postulated by large-body physics presupposes the determinism of subatomic physics. Of course it may conceivably be found in future that completely reliable predictions can be made of the behaviour of persons and of fundamental particles; but so long as the admitted determinism (for practical purposes) of aggregates of these persons and particles can be explained on the basis of the merely probable behaviour of their constituent entities, to say that ultimately determinism will be found to apply to them too seems little more than a declaration of faith. There is a serious question, of course, whether the non-determinism of such large-scale entities as men can depend, for practical purposes, on the indeterminism of subatomic particles. This argument requires a scientific expertise I do not possess; suffice it to say that according to some reputable scientists, such dependence is possible.[28]

So far my arguments concerning determinism and libertarianism have been mainly defensive; I have not tried to refute determinism, but only to show that some philosophical and scientific arguments alleged to prove it, or at least to make it highly plausible, can be refuted. My more aggressive attempt to demonstrate that determinism is inconsistent with Christian theism and with moral responsibility, as these are usually conceived, and perhaps with psychoanalysis as generally understood, may not, even if valid, unduly worry determinists. But there are other difficulties more intrinsic to the determinist position. Rational beings characteristically behave in accordance with plans which they believe to be appropriate to their situation. Material objects behave according to laws which the scientist can discover. There is an interesting question how these forms of explanation fit together in the case of human beings, who are, of course, both material objects and rational beings. One obvious solution is that rational choices are made from possibilities which are real in that, given the causal preconditions, any one of them might have occurred. This solution is open to the libertarian, but closed to the determinist, who does not believe that there are real possibilities of this kind. For him, it seems to me, there are two possible solutions. Either all propositions about acting for reasons can be reduced to propositions about behaving owing to the operation of causes, in that any statement of the first type can be shown to be identical in meaning with statements of the second; or there is no logical connection between acting for reasons and behaving owing to the operation of causes, though the former depends entirely upon the latter. To take the former alternative: I cannot see how one would begin to show that, for example, "I drew that figure on the paper to demonstrate the truth of Pythagoras' theorem" is really *identical in meaning* with a series of statements about electrical currents running through nerves and chemical reactions at synapses. The latter alternative seems to lead to the even more implausible conclusion that it is just by a colossal coincidence (or perhaps by a special divine providence?) that a series of electrical and chemical events, obeying the laws intrinsic to such things, really direct our reasoning, which appears to follow very different principles; that our reasoning is really an epiphenomenon of these brain-processes, which can have no relation to truth and plausibility such as it is proper for reasoning to have.

If this account of human freedom is at all correct, light is thrown on a suggestion of Plato in the *Phaedrus*, that it is of the essence of souls to move bodies, and of bodies to be moved. On this account of the matter, God must be a soul and not a body, in that he moves all else, without himself being moved by anything; whereas men are largely determined by the forces which act upon them. However, men also have their margin of freedom, within which to act this way or that is up to them. Men are (or have) souls as well as bodies in the sense that they move independently of being moved, act independently of being acted upon. (Perhaps the proposition that man is made in the image of God may be interpreted, not wholly fancifully, in this sense;[29] whereas God is the wholly undetermined determiner of all else, man is also an undetermined determiner within a very narrow scope.) One might have to speculate on what it would be for souls without bodies to exist, or on what it would be for us to become aware of their existence, if there were not to hand so many alleged examples—for instance, from the literature on poltergeists.[30] Poltergeists are said to betray their existence by the fact that furniture is shifted and clatters are caused in a way that is not accountable in any normal manner, but as though the purpose of these events were to annoy or to attract attention; the alleged agents, however, are themselves invisible and intangible. The possibility, such as it is, that all the alleged evidence for the actual occurrence of such things is a result of error or deceit, is not to the point. The conceivability of the existence of disembodied souls is evident if, given that such phenomena are imaginable and whether they actually take place or not, the only way to make sense of them is in terms of the activity of such entities.

I have argued the virtual necessity of the libertarian doctrine for Christian theism, and also for its possibility and plausibility in spite of philosophical and scientific objections. Yet in fact, among representative Christian (and *a fortiori* Islamic) thinkers, there has been at least as much polemic against the exaggeration of the power and scope of human freedom as against determinism.[31] Augustine says "Let us not defend grace in such a way as to seem to make away with free will. On the other hand, we may not assert freedom of will in such manner as in our impious pride to be judged ungrateful for the grace of God."[32] It might be argued, with Pelagius and his followers, that the help which God gives to man in order that he may be saved consists of no more than originally creating him with free will, giving him commands to follow and promises and threats to induce him to do so, and setting him a good example in Christ. This theory has been rejected by the Church at large as greatly exaggerating the extent of human freedom. That man can save himself by his own efforts goes against much New Testament teaching, and is also belied by the experience of many people that they are often impotent in their struggle against moral failings, and thus, when they do overcome them, that they rely largely on forces outside themselves. Augustine, the great opponent of Pelagius, had personal experience of this, and could quote Paul: "The good which I want to do, I fail to do; but what I do is the wrong which is against my will."[33] It must be said that everything in contemporary psychology and sociology supports Augustine against Pelagianism, even if the existence of free-will is not disproved;[34] the determining power of constitution, upbringing and circumstances upon us is enormous. Those who do not thank God for such virtue as they think they possess ought at least to thank their good luck.

Pelagius and Calvin represent the extreme positions which may be taken up on the relation of divine grace to free human action. The question is whether there is really any consistently tenable mediating position. The history of the controversy might well make one conclude that there is not. But simply to abandon the problem, while insisting all the same that one must not be either a Calvinist or a Pelagian, is to invite the jibe that the Christian faith is not so much a divine mystery as a conceptual muddle.

No better illustration can be found of the difficulty than the controversy about grace which took place in the Catholic Church in the sixteenth and seventeenth centuries. Both Calvinism and Pelagianism were admitted to be heretical; the problem was to find a mediating account. Two principal solutions were proposed, one by Molina the Jesuit, which started from human free will and tried to accommodate God's grace to that; the second by Bañez the Dominican, who approached the problem from the opposite end. Two technical terms played a part in the controversy, *sufficient grace* and *efficacious grace*. By efficacious grace was meant that action by God upon a man by which he is actually enabled to perform good deeds and is brought ultimately to heaven. By sufficient grace was meant the help which God offers to all men (whether they accept it or not) which is sufficient to save them, if they accept it. Molina said there was no intrinsic difference between the two sorts of grace; that merely sufficient grace became efficacious grace if the believer freely accepted it. Bañez held, on the contrary, that God himself turned sufficient grace into efficacious grace in the case of those who were actually saved. The Jesuit party which supported Molina complained that, if God had so to speak to add something from his side in order to make sufficient grace efficacious, one might just as well deny that merely sufficient grace was sufficient at all; thus the Dominican position was really Calvinist. In fact the Jansenists (Catholics who in effect took the Calvinist position in this matter) actually used to pray to God to deliver them from merely sufficient grace. Everyone else agreed that the implications of such a prayer were as absurd as they were blasphemous; but it seemed to the Jesuits that, on the premisses upheld by the Dominicans, one might just as well pray thus. On the other hand, the Dominicans argued that if one accepted the Jesuit premisses, since everything in effect seemed to depend on a man's free option for or against salvation, one might just as well be a Pelagian. Further, the Molinist position did not at all do justice to the central Christian view that God was pre-eminently active in the words and deeds of the sanctified (cf. Phil. 2.13). If the difference between the sanctified and the un-sanctified is due only to the efforts of the sanctified, what room is there for that gratitude to God which ought above all to characterize the life of the saint?

Of the two views, the Molinist seems to give full scope to the essential Christian doctrine of human responsibility for sin, at the apparent expense of the equally central Christian doctrine that men are saved by the grace of God; while the Bannezian has just the opposite advantage and disadvantage. One is driven to the perhaps odd conclusion that the merits and eternal reward of the saints are due to God, while at the same time the sins and consequent damnation of the reprobate are due to them alone. Augustine gives a hint of this when he says that free will is enough to account for evil, but for good can do nothing unless assisted by grace.[35] On this view salvation is due to total self-surrender to the grace of God, in such a way that both merit and reward are from him; while damnation is due to a refusal of this grace (which might perhaps be interpreted in concrete terms as a deliberate turning away from the good as one sees it) and both demerits and punishment are a result of this refusal. If this is the case, both sides in the Molinist-Bannezian dispute are partly right and partly wrong; the Bannezians are wrong in assuming that the difference between merely sufficient and efficacious grace consists in an additional shove imparted to the human soul by God, the Molinists in assuming in effect that divine grace is equally active in the bad as the good, only that the bad have contributed their refusal, the good their acceptance. Perhaps the dilemma may be resolved if one says that, in the case of those who are ultimately saved, God's grace in external circumstance co-operates with God-given power to respond appropriately; in the case of the damned, there is the same pressure of external events working towards salvation, and the same God-given power, but in this case the creature refuses of its own free will. Who has actually accepted (except, according to Catholics, in the case of the canonized saints), and who has refused, the proffered grace of God, we have no means of knowing. Though the presumption is certainly the opposite, Hitler, for all we know, may have used the opportunities he was given to better effect than Gandhi. That a man is, socially speaking, a criminal, may be written into his genetic code; but whether he accepts the grace of God cannot be so.

The discussion of grace makes it possible to give an answer to the question raised in the first chapter; of how it is possible for God to act in and through the actions of free rational agents without abrogating their freedom. The actions of those who make obedient use of the powers God has given them, and respond obediently to him to what happens to them as they live their lives, are pre-eminently God's actions; whereas the actions of those who deliberately rebel against God, though not God's actions so far as they are rebellious, are yet his actions in that they are employed by him in such a way as to be instrumental in bringing about his kingdom of justice and happiness. Good and bad men alike are instrumental in God's providence, the good by deliberate intention to do what is good, the wicked in spite of themselves. As Augustine writes: "As God is the best creator of good natures, so is he the just disposer of evil wills: that when they use good natures ill, he may use the evil wills well. . . . He caused that the devil's . . . temptations might confirm his saints, whom the other sought to injure."[36] Aquinas says that God, as first cause acting through the secondary causes which constitute the created world, respects the nature of each; and so in acting through free rational creatures does not abrogate their freedom.[37] It may be concluded that, of all the events of which the created world consists, the acts of good rational creatures are most pre-eminently God's actions, while those of rebellious rational creatures are the least so; yet even these remain so, in that they are instrumental in bringing about the ultimate good for the universe willed by God. What is involved in this conception will be worked out further in the discussion of providence and evil.

The account of grace which I have given has been somewhat abstract; very little reference has so far been made to the particular aspects of people's experience which make them wish to talk in terms of God's grace. It has been the experience of those whom Christians have called saints that, precisely in those actions which others have called heroically good, they have felt that what they did was not due to their own power or virtue but to God acting through them. And Christians at large find that they seem to gain a strength in mastering temptations and difficulties, and a serenity and resilience in misery, as a result of that life with God of which prayer is the characteristic expression. But it is important not to conceive grace exclusively in terms of experiences like this, since everything that happens to him is properly regarded by a Christian as part of the gracious activity of God guiding him towards ultimate salvation.[38]

The mediating position on grace, neither Calvinist nor Pelagian, neither denying human liberty nor over-emphasizing it, is perhaps most adequately and systematically set out by Aquinas. He holds that while a man is unable of himself to acquire or deserve grace and thus do good deeds, he can nevertheless stop himself from receiving grace. "To obstruct or not to obstruct the entrance of divine grace, this lies in the power of a man's own free will; if he does so, he is not unfairly blamed. God for his part is ready to give grace to all."[39] The possibility of receiving the grace of God, and so being restored to good, remains for each man on earth, however much he has sinned; but every bad voluntary action increases the tendency towards evil and decreases that towards good.[40]

This analysis of the gravity of the state of sin in terms of probability that one will act wrongly in future, a probability which never reaches certainty in this life, is reminiscent of the place of probability in contemporary physics as usually interpreted. The thesis of some physicists, that these probabilities will reveal underlying necessities when more is known, is parallel to the Hobbesian position that human freedom, in the radical sense, disappears in as far as the causal preconditions of action are fully known. But these cases have to be proved, and nothing like proof is so far available. The fact that knowledge of the causal preconditioning of a human agent tends to narrow the options held to be available for him does not prove that, once all the preconditions are known, the range of actions available to him will be reduced to the one which he does in fact perform. But the Christian theology of grace agrees with recent psychological and sociological evidence that the individual's real freedom of manoeuvre is at least severely limited, and that no one but the omniscient has material for any but the most tentative praise or blame. There is impressive scientific as well as theological ground for the maxim "Judge not, that ye be not judged".[41]

The account of human freedom which I have given has been held in many quarters to be inconsistent with two central theistic doctrines—those of God's omniscience and providence. The conviction of God's unfailing providence led Calvin and Jonathan Edwards to deny human freedom in any but the curtailed sense that in "free" actions men are necessitated but not externally constrained; on the other hand Charles Hartshorne, seeking to defend theism while asserting a more radical doctrine of human freedom, has as a consequence felt compelled to deny the doctrine of God's foreknowledge.[42] If God knows all future contingencies (so the argument runs), they cannot but come to pass as he knows they will. But "free" human actions are among these contingencies. Consequently, given God's foreknowledge, "free" human actions in the future cannot be other than they are. And since the omniscient God must have known the whole course of world events from the beginning, no human action could ever have been otherwise than it was. Confronted with this apparent choice between God's omniscience and providence on the one hand and real human freedom on the other, Hartshorne affirms real human freedom at the expense of divine omniscience and providence, while Calvin and Edwards affirm divine omniscience and providence at the expense of real human freedom.

The argument underlying both positions, that divine omniscience and providence are inconsistent with what I have called real human freedom, is set out at length by Jonathan Edwards.[43] God as the Bible presents him, Edwards insists, knows from the beginning everything which is to happen in the world. Since God foreknows every event, including those subject to human will, every event must necessarily take place according to this foreknowledge. "If there be any infallible knowledge of future volitions, the event is necessary; or, in other words . . . , it is impossible but that the event should come to pass." The only alternative is that God is ignorant of future events, and hence that world history may come out contrary to his plan. "If this notion of God's ignorance of the future volitions of moral agents be thoroughly considered in its consequences, it will appear to follow from it, that God, after he had made the world, was liable to be wholly frustrated of his end in the creation of it." But if God knows the future, this can only be because it must infallibly fall out as it does by the working of causal laws from states of affairs obtaining in the past and present; after all, there is no other way in which even God could know it *now*. " 'Tis impossible for a thing to be certainly known to any intellect without evidence. To suppose otherwise, implies a contradiction: because for a thing to be certainly known to any understanding is for it to be evident to that understanding . . . But no understanding, created or increated, can see evidence where there is none . . . But if there be any future event, whose existence is . . . without . . . necessity, the future existence of that event is absolutely without evidence."[44]

Edwards assumes that God, like a human scientist, knows events which are now future through inference by means of causal laws from events of the past and present. It is precisely this supposition which is denied by Aquinas, who was following here a much earlier tradition. Aquinas admits that if the future were wholly knowable, even by God, *as* future—and such knowledge is certainly through inference from the present state of affairs by means of causal laws—then indeed it would be predetermined. But Aquinas denies that it is by such means that God knows what is now future. His conception of divine knowledge is derived from Boethius, who wrote: "If you reflect on the immediate confrontation by which God discerns all things, you will judge that it is not foreknowledge of something as future, but rather knowledge of a never failing present. For which reason it is called not previdence but providence, because it is set far above the lowly details of the world and sees all things as though from the highest summit. . . . Those future events which proceed from free will God sees as present."[45] Boethius thus conceives of God as enjoying a vantage-point over space and time, analogous to that which a human observer may have over a wide range of space.

Aquinas claims that God knows in eternity all events, whether past, present, or future from our point of view; those that are necessitated by their preconditions as so necessitated, those that are not so necessitated (like the free acts of men and angels) as not so necessitated.[46] Strictly speaking, he says, God as an eternal being does not *fore*know at all; he *knows* (timelessly). On this view, God knows what will happen tomorrow. But he does not strictly speaking *know today* what will happen tomorrow, let alone, as Edwards assumes, know today what will happen tomorrow by inference from what happens today together with the laws of nature. An eternal being knows, but cannot foreknow; since foreknowledge strictly speaking involves inference of the kind I have described, and the need to depend on inference for such knowledge is a limitation proper to temporal beings. The human need to supplement knowledge by acquaintance with inference, in order to anticipate the future, is part and parcel of what it is to be a spatio-temporal creature, albeit a rational one; there is no reason to believe that such restrictions apply to the knowledge enjoyed by the being whose activity itself constitutes the world of space and time, rather than being conditioned by it.[47]

I think it is true that, if God exists and is in the proper sense omniscient, then either determinism is inevitable, or God's knowledge must be conceived as outside time in something like the way I have outlined. There are certainly difficulties and obscurities in this conception; but it is by no means clear to me that it is fundamentally incoherent.

3 EVIL

The most serious objection to theism can be briefly stated. God is claimed to be both all-powerful and infinitely good. Yet there is evil and suffering in the world which he is supposed to have created. Now it is part of the meaning of the word "good", at least as applied to rational agents, that a good being does not permit evil to occur in those states of affairs which are under his control, or at least that, when he does so, it should be as a means to the bringing about of a greater good than could be brought about without the evil. But that God has to use evil means to bring about good ends conflicts with the doctrine of his omnipotence. Consequently, since there is evil in the world, and since evil cannot for an omnipotent being be a necessary means of bringing about a greater good than would otherwise be possible, the universe cannot have been created by a being who is both omnipotent and wholly good. That the universe is as we find it to be is consistent, perhaps, with its creation by a God who is all-powerful but not absolutely good, or absolutely good but not all-powerful; but it is not compatible with its creation by a God who is both all-good and all-powerful, as God is believed to be by Christians.

The treatment of the problem of evil in Barth's *Dogmatics* is peculiar in that it does not so much provide or even adumbrate answers to these well-known difficulties, as refuse to do so. The reason which Barth gives for this is that any systematic explanation of evil will lessen its gravity, and especially man's culpability as a sinner. The task of the theologian, as Barth sees it, is not to create a philosophically coherent system, but to state the truth about God's creation as it is shown to be by the Word of God in Scripture. And the Word of God proclaims that creation has become broken and self-contradictory; this brokenness should therefore be reflected in theological discourse.[1] Sin is a monstrous and utterly irrational pact by men with those forces which resist God's creation and which constantly threaten it.[2] It may naturally be asked what is the nature of this mysterious being or realm of beings which threatens God's creation. It can hardly be identified with God, since its very essence is to resist his creative and gracious purposes. On the other hand, Barth will not allow that it is itself a creature or creatures; indeed it resists God by the perversion and destruction of creatures. Barth calls it "nothingness", and yet affirms its dire effectiveness; he says it is not simply non-existent, but "is" in a peculiar manner of its own, different alike from the being of God and of his creatures—essentially an opposition to God and a threat to creatures.[3] This "nothingness" consists of the possibilities which God rejected in creating the world as he did.[4] The question of *why* man made and makes an alliance with evil must not be asked. We must not say even that God made man *capable* of succumbing to sin; this would mitigate the total wickedness and perversity of man's rebellion against God. All we can say is that man has sinned and does sin.[5]

The objections to Barth's position on this matter spring to the eye; it is difficult to see how, outside the magnificent intellectual structure of the *Dogmatics* as a whole, they could carry conviction with anyone. In his exposition of the Christian doctrines of creation and sin, Barth asserts two propositions which certainly contradict one another: that God created man such that he was not capable of falling into sin; and that man did fall into sin. Barth's motive in constructing this strange account is to maintain the full responsibility of man for his sin. But to *explain* how an action was performed, as opposed to explaining how an action could not have been performed in any other way than it was, is not to *excuse* the agent of that action.[6] To say that an action is irrational, again, is not to say that it is inexplicable; it is to say that to explain it is not in this case to provide good reasons which motivated the agent in doing it. A man who spoils his own chances of happiness or advancement by succumbing to impulses of lust or rudeness is "irrational" in this sense; but his actions on one basis or the other are not inexplicable. Of course one may without contradiction say that an event or action is inexplicable, at any rate in relation to presently available knowledge; but Barth goes further than this. He actually proposes a theory which rules out the possibility of the action which he says is "irrational", while acknowledging that the kind of action in question, rebellion against God, is in fact universal. If God created man so that it was not possible for man to fall into sin, man did not do so. But man did so. Therefore, God did not create man so that he was not capable of falling into sin. No argument could be more conclusive than that. To hold both of the two propositions which Barth here insists on holding is to abandon all claims to rationality. It is of no use whatever to claim that, in this case, a broken reality has to be described in broken discourse.[7] If a man contradicts himself, he is not describing a contradictory reality, but failing to describe reality at all.

It is certainly the case that theological discourse must be, of its very essence, paradoxical, since it depends on the possibility of applying to God epithets and descriptions whose primary application is to the things and persons of our familiar world. But the difference between paradox and nonsense is that, in the case of paradox, where I say that A is at the same time X and not X, I imply that X is not precisely delimited in meaning; A is thus X in one sense, but not in another. One might say that, for Christians, Christ both is and is not a priest and a king. The early Christians did not proclaim Christ's priestly office and kingly rule quite in the same sense as these would be understood by the orthodox Jews of their time; on the other hand, the significance of "king" and "priest" was not wholly other as applied to him than as understood by them. Catullus, when he confessed that he at once loved and hated the same woman, described paradoxically and so very precisely a state which was in a sense love, in a sense just the opposite. But a straight contradiction, in which a proposition of unambiguous meaning is at once asserted and denied, cannot be a description of anything. Theologians have as much right as poets to use paradox as a way of expressing what they have to say; but they ought to be at pains to make clear the distinction between an enlightening paradox and a contradiction.[8] And the problem of evil for the theist is nothing else than that to say at once that the universe is the work of an omnipotent and perfectly good God, and that there is a great deal of evil in it, is at least at first sight a contradiction.

It has been said, even by Christian writers, that Christianity provides no solution for the problem of evil.[9] This admission is quite proper for them in one sense, that Christians as such are not committed to any one particular detailed account of how evil came into the world. But in another sense it is certainly not. It is not possible to be both honestly and clear-sightedly a Christian, and to hold that while there is evil in the world Christian belief excludes the very possibility of there being evil in the world. To propound *that* kind of paradox is simply to make a fool of God.

The solution to the problem which might be called classical is that of Aquinas, who in this matter as in so many others was building on foundations laid by his predecessors, particularly St Augustine. All existent beings, according to Aquinas, are as such good; a thing is only bad so far as it fails to be what it ought to be, just as the sort of thing that it is. Evil, in other words, is essentially "privation", or (as it might be better to say in contemporary terms) deficiency. To be incapable of sight is not a defect in a stone, since a stone is not the sort of thing that ought to be able to see; but it is a defect in a sheep or a man. (It is typical of Aquinas that he subsumes all kinds of evil, both physical and moral, under one very general metaphysical concept. This seems to me to correspond to the Gospels, where the forgiveness of sins and the cure of disease are both represented as aspects of Christ's onslaught on the powers of evil.) It is wrong to say that God "created" evil, since evil is not a "thing" for God to have created; but the possibility of being deficient in a quality one should have is inherent in being a creature. The existence of corruptible beings brings evil in its train.[10] Evil being essentially a lack, a failure by something to be what it ought to be, and beings as such being essentially good, there must be more good than evil in the universe, since evil only exists as parasitic on good.[11]

God allows the corruptions and defects of individual things for the good of the universe as a whole.[12] Often a thing may not be able to realize its own nature fully without damaging something else. Thus the occurrence of each kind of evil is permitted for the realization of another kind of good.

> The whole itself, the universe of creatures, is better and the more perfect for the things that can fall short in goodness, and which sometimes do fall short in the event without God preventing them. It happens thus, for . . . the role of Providence is not to regiment but to respect nature. What may fail should fail sometimes. Many good things would be missed if God permitted no evil to exist: fire would not burn unless air were consumed, lions would not thrive unless asses were killed, nor would just retribution be inflicted and long-suffering patience praised but for the iniquity of persecution.[13]

The last point is reminiscent of John Hick's argument that intense physical evil may be worthwhile as evoking great moral goodness in man.[14] The suggestion that wickedness is worthwhile for the retribution inflicted on it I find both unpalatable and unconvincing. However, the general line of argument, that some good ends can be realized only by the actuality of some kinds of evil and at least the real possibility of other kinds, is fairly clear and not evidently absurd.

The manner in which evil in the parts of the world may contribute to the good of the world as a whole may be set out in aesthetic rather than moral terms; St Augustine's theodicy is largely of this type. In ordering the world, God, according to Augustine's account, is like a great poet or dramatist, whose work as a whole is better if all degrees of worth are present in it, the very bad to set off by contrast the very good. The universe as a whole would not necessarily be the better if all the bad or inferior creatures in it were better than or superior to what they are. (This involves the paradox to which G. E. Moore drew attention in *Principia Ethica*,[15] that the value of some kinds of a whole is not directly proportionate to the value of their parts.) "God would never have foreknown vice in any work of his, angel or man, but that he knew in like manner what good use to put it unto, so making the world's course, like a fair poem, more gracious by antithetic figures".[16] And things which are in fact often physically harmful to man, such as fire, cold, and wild animals, are not only an additional beauty in the context of the universe as a whole, but also harm men less when used in the right way. (Augustine held that the greater part of man's susceptibility to physical suffering was due to his lapse into moral evil—a view which would be far more difficult to maintain in our time than in his.)[17] However, Augustine does not rely entirely on this aesthetic analogy; he also declares, in the manner of Aquinas and Hick, that the ultimate effect of physical and moral evil may be to test and strengthen the moral goodness of some creatures.

According to Aquinas, evil as deficiency may affect a thing in two ways, in itself or in its operation. Physical evil is evil of the first kind, as when an animal is killed or maimed. As to operation, there may be in anything "a gap in the proper activity, either by non-performance or failure in execution or direction".[18] A thing may either fail to function as it should at all, or the function may be deficient in itself or exercised on an inappropriate object. An animal or man, for example, which is built to thrive on foods of certain kinds, may either fail to eat at all, or fail to complete the process of eating by digesting food, or eat the wrong kind of food. All of these sorts of behaviour would be different kinds of deficiency in the function of eating. Sin is a defect in the proper operation of a rational being; the sinful individual is one certain of whose proper functions are not exercised at all, or exercised in the wrong way, or applied to the wrong objects. For instance, a man as such has an intelligence which he ought to develop; but he may get so obsessed with sensual pleasure as to let his intelligence atrophy, or he may devote it to trivial things at the expense of more important ones, or he may exercise it in the interests of malice. Now God may properly be said to cause, at least indirectly, that kind of evil which comes about through one creature realizing its nature properly but at the expense of another. He makes kestrels thrive at the expense of mice, hydras at the expense of water-fleas. But when a being is really free, as rational beings are free, to realize its proper function appropriately or not to do so, if it does not do so, this failure can not be attributed to God. Certainly God is responsible for the *possibility* of the failure; but this is not to imply that he is responsible for the failure itself. Since moral evil is of this kind, God cannot be said to bring it about, though he can be said to bring about at least some physical evil.[19]

Not that even a being free to realize its proper nature, or not to do so, can perform an evil action simply as such; it must be done with a view to some good or other. "The evil that is the constitutive difference in moral matters is a particular good joined to the privation of another good; the end sought by the intemperate man is not the loss of the benefit of reason, but sense-delight involving rational disorder."[20] To do wrong, in other words, is to realize an inferior good at the expense of a greater. To fulfil one's desire is as such good; it is only when fulfilment of an immediate desire is inimical to the achievement of one's long-term happiness, in this life or hereafter, that it is evil. Every act of sin increases the propensity to sin; however, no amount of sinning will make it absolutely necessary for the sinner to go on sinning, and the embracing of virtue impossible for him. "Even were the contrary disposition piled up indefinitely, the instinct for right action would be but indefinitely weakened, not wholly destroyed."[21] Otherwise the sinner would become no longer responsible for his sinful acts and consequently, since sin depends logically on responsibility, he would no longer be a sinner. The way the propensity to sin may be indefinitely increased, without ever reaching absolute compulsion, may be illustrated by a mathematical analogy; however many times you divide a number by half, you never reach absolute zero. So it is with a man's diminishing of his freedom by repeated acts of sin.[22]

Aquinas' account of the relation of God to the evil in his creation may thus be summed up as follows. Four types of state of affairs may be distinguished: (*a*) what God wills to happen for its own sake; (*b*) what he wills to happen for the sake of something else; (*c*) what he permits to happen; and (*d*) what he absolutely wills not to happen. Evil is to be conceived in terms of deficiency; a thing is bad to the degree that it lacks qualities which, as a thing of its kind, it ought to have. A thing may become deficient either in itself, or in its function; physical evil is a deficiency of the first kind, while moral evil (which is the impairment of a function proper to rational creatures) is one of the second kind. Physical evil in the creature is brought about by God for the good of some other creature, for the good of the universe as a whole, or for the chastisement or ultimate good of rebellious rational agents. God is directly responsible for physical evil as he is not for moral evil, which he merely permits. This he does because it is better that there should exist creatures free either to fall from moral rectitude or to maintain it, than that all creatures should obey God of necessity; and what *can* fail sometimes *will*. Thus, in fine, the good of creatures, or the realizing by each of them of its full potential, is directly willed by God (*a*); the impairment of some creatures is brought about for the good of others and of the creation as a whole (*b*); it is better that there should be beings free to do good or to fail to do it than that there should be none such; and hence some do fail (*c*). What God absolutely wills not to happen, of course, cannot do so, since he is omnipotent (*d*).

For Aquinas, then, God has supreme "metaphysical" goodness (as one might put it) in that he is not subject to the deficiency and decay which are the fate of the creatures of the world; he has supreme aesthetic goodness in that contemplation of him gives intense and unalloyed delight;[23] and he has moral goodness in that he brings about physical evil, and permits moral evil, only as a means to greater good than would otherwise be possible. At least two kinds of objection may be made: (*a*) that a being cannot be both omnipotent and utterly good who uses evil, or at least as much evil as there is in the world, to bring about good; (*b*) that, in the case of an omnipotent and omniscient creator, a real distinction between what he actively wills and what he merely permits is impossible to make. Both points have been argued very forcefully in an article by J. L. Mackie.[24] This article is a remarkably concise and lucid statement of the problem of evil, together with a useful criticism of the ways in which theists commonly try to resolve it. I shall first outline Mackie's argument, and then try to suggest how a theist might counter it.

Mackie very rightly says that, if the problem of evil is really unanswerable for theists, the fact is much more damaging to their position than failure of the proofs for the existence of God; since it shows that the characteristic belief of theists not only *cannot* be *proved*, but *can be disproved*. The problem (he goes on) can be very summarily stated: "God is omnipotent; God is wholly good; and yet evil exists." Two other subsidiary principles will bring out that the apparent contradiction is real, and hence that the problem of evil is insoluble for the theist; first, that "good is opposed to evil, *in such a way that a good thing always eliminates evil as far as it can*";[25] second, that an omnipotent being can do anything whatever. Of course, the problem of evil is quite soluble for any theist who says that God is not quite omnipotent, or not wholly good, or that evil does not exist; but most theists fail to make concessions of this kind. On the contrary, "there are many so-called solutions which purport to remove the contradiction without removing any of its constituent propositions. These must be fallacious, as we can see from the very statement of the problem, but it is not so easy to see in each case precisely where the fallacy lies." On examination, it is found that the fallacy always has the following general form: "in order to solve the problem one (or perhaps more) of its constituent propositions is given up, but in such a way that it appears to have been retained, and can therefore be asserted without qualification in other contexts".[26]

Mackie investigates four such solutions. First, " 'Good cannot exist without evil', or 'Evil is necessary as a counterpart to good' ". If what is claimed here is that the existence of evil is *logically* necessary to the existence of the good, it may be admitted that this does not impugn God's omnipotence as bearing only on what is *causally* possible. But surely, even so, the existence of a very small amount of real evil would be enough—at least, less than the vast amount of evil generally admitted to exist in the world. Second,

"Evil is necessary as a means to good". This evidently involves a severe restriction of God's power, since it follows that he is subject to certain causal laws. It is certainly inconsistent with his "omnipotence" on any usual understanding of the term.[27]

The third solution Mackie considers is that "the universe is better with some evil in it than it could be if there were no evil". This suggestion may be developed in terms of an aesthetic analogy —that ugly parts may contribute positively to the beauty of a picture as a whole, or discords to that of a piece of music. Alternatively, appeal may be made to the idea of progress, and the claim put forward "that the gradual overcoming of evil by good is really a finer thing than would be the eternal and unchallenged supremacy of good". On this view the existence of pain and disease renders possible moral qualities of heroism, sympathy, and benevolence, displayed in the overcoming of these evils, which would not be logically possible without them. In order that what is at issue here may be clarified, a distinction can be made between first-order good or "good (1)" (happiness, pleasure, etc.), and second-order good or "good (2)" (heroism, sympathy, etc.). Expressed in these terms, the proposed solution is that God does not desire unconditionally to promote first-order good, which would mean that he could not allow the first-order evils of pain and disease to exist; but that he wishes to promote second-order good, that is to say, the moral qualities in human agents acquired in the overcoming of first-order evil and the replacing of it with the first-order good. God himself, it must be pointed out, can on this view be "good" only in yet a third way—that of aiming to bring about second-order goodness. He certainly cannot himself have second-order goodness, since he does not exert himself to get rid of pain and disease and to promote pleasure and happiness. It is also to be noted that good and evil according to this solution are not, as according to one of the initial suppositions they are, unequivocally opposed to and destructive of one another; they are related in a more complex way.[28]

Mackie admits the plausibility and subtlety of this solution, but submits an objection which he thinks is fatal.

Our analysis shows clearly the possibility of the existence of a *second* order evil, an evil (2) contrasting with good (2) as evil (1) contrasts with good (1). This would include malevolence, cruelty, callousness, cowardice, and states in which good (1) is decreasing and evil (1) increasing.

And just as good (2) is held to be the important kind of good, that kind that God is concerned to promote, so evil (2) will, by analogy, be the important kind of evil, the kind which God, if he were wholly good and omnipotent, would eliminate. And yet evil (2) plainly exists. . . . Against this form of the problem the present solution is useless.

And even if one could justify such second-order goods by their contribution to third-order good, the problem would only recur on that level—and thus it is hard to see how the theist could avoid an infinite regress if he went on arguing along these lines; every appeal he made to good of order n+1, to justify evil of order n, could be countered by assertion of the existence of evil of order n+1.[29]

The fourth solution, that "Evil is due to human freewill", may be used in conjunction with the third: "first-order evil (e.g. pain) may be justified as a logically necessary component in second-order good (e.g. sympathy) while second-order evil (e.g. cruelty) is not *justified*, but is so ascribed to human beings that God cannot be held responsible for it." This solution, he admits, is not impugned by his criticism of the preceding one. "To explain why a wholly good God gave men freewill although it would lead to some important evils, it must be argued that it is better on the whole that men should act freely, and sometimes err, than that they should be innocent automata, acting rightly in a wholly determined way. . . . I think that this solution is unsatisfying *primarily because of the incoherence of the notion of the freedom of the will.*"[30] Even given that the actual making of some wrong choices is a necessary consequence of freedom, such freedom in action can scarcely amount to anything but sheer randomness—as would be the case if the postulated "free" actions were not determined by the characters of those who performed them. And even if such random action were possible, it is difficult to see how it could be worthwhile. "What value or merit would there be in free choices if there were *random* actions which were not *determined by the nature of the agent*?"[31]

I have already tried to show at some length that the notion of free will is perfectly coherent, and that the premiss on which Mackie founds his objection to it, that every event which is not predetermined is random, is false.[32] It seems to me that a solution is to be found partly on the assumption that God has created human (and perhaps angelic) agents with a real freedom such as I have described, and partly by a modification of some suggestions which Mackie himself makes in relation to the third solution which he mentions. I shall assume, as Mackie concedes may be legitimate in the context of this solution, that the relation between good and evil is not such that a good thing (of whatever kind) must eliminate evil (of whatever kind) as far as it can. It will be appropriate, for my own purposes, to talk in terms of "types" rather than "orders" of good and evil, since what would naturally be described as "third-order" good or evil, and is so described by Mackie, will be included, for reasons that will appear, in my second type. Suppose that we agree with Mackie on the characterization of first-type good (pleasure and happiness) and first-type evil (pain and disease). We will, however, modify his account of second-type good in such a way that it will consist in the disposition not only to promote first-type good and to diminish first-type evil, but also to strive against real possibilities of second-type evil in oneself, and real second-type evil in others—and similarly with promoting second-order good. Second-type evil, as well as promoting first-type evil and resisting first-type good, will strive against second-type good. Let us now define third-type good as that moral goodness in an agent which will ultimately prevail over real possibilities of second-type evil in the agent himself, and over all first- and second-type evil with which it comes into conflict in the world. Now suppose that the existence of third-type good, which logically entails the real existence of first-type evil and at least the possibility of second-type evil, is the absolute purpose of God. Now, it is *possible* that there might be third-type evil, i.e. that which ultimately prevails in the destruction of good; or that there should be no good or evil of the third type. But it is part of the faith of most theists that there is in fact no evil of this third type, but that there is good—in other words, that moral good will ultimately prevail. Hence Mackie's infinite regress is avoided.

That God's will is the bringing into being of what I call third-type good is not a mere logical possibility, worked out to evade Mackie's strictures; it seems to be the teaching of the New Testament. According to St John's Gospel, Jesus Christ claims to have overcome the world;[33] that is to say, by the power available through him, men may be brought to that third-type goodness which prevails over second- and first-type evils.

That the existence of human moral good does logically involve a general situation containing evil as well as good has been argued by Ninian Smart.[34] According to him, men made incapable of evil actions, who never had to overcome impulses of selfishness, cruelty, or cowardice, could not possibly be "good" in anything like the sense in which we are accustomed to use the term of human beings; indeed, it may be wondered in what sense they could be "men" at all. One may say of such abstract possibilities as the existence of men built wholly good what Flew says of theological propositions—that they are subject to death by a thousand qualifications.[35] These qualifications have inevitably to be made when the full implications of these abstract "possibilities" are worked out.

> The concept *goodness* is applied to beings of a certain sort, beings who are liable to temptation, possess inclinations, have fears, tend to assert themselves and so forth; and . . . if they were to be immunized from evil they would have to be built in a different way. But it soon becomes apparent that to rebuild them would mean that the ascription of goodness would become unintelligible, for the reasons why men are called good and bad have a connection with human nature as it is empirically discovered to be. Moral utterance is embedded in the cosmic status quo.

An interesting incidental feature of this argument is that, as Smart points out, it does not presuppose the falsity of determinism.

Applying Smart's arguments to Mackie's objections, then, the theist might maintain that God wills to bring into being third-type good, for which it is logically necessary for him to bring about first-type evil and at least to allow second-type evil. The reality of the distinction between what God brings about and what he merely allows depends, of course, on the reality of that kind of radical freedom the possibility of which I defended in the previous chapter.

So far, in argument with Mackie, I have been mainly concerned with the general question of what could be meant, if anything, by calling a being both all-powerful and all-good while admitting that he is responsible for a universe which has a great deal of evil in it. But it seems worthwhile also to approach the question from another direction and to inquire, when believers have ascribed both omnipotence and absolute goodness to God, what in detail they have attributed to him and expected from him in so doing. As in the case of other attributes of God,[36] it seems appropriate to elucidate what is meant by the goodness of God by reference to more particular qualities, actions, and dispositions which believers have ascribed to him. The question of God's goodness, as thus approached, is not primarily "what *could* be meant by calling God good?", but rather "what *has* actually been meant by people who have called God good?"

In calling God good, Christians have hoped in future to "see" or "meet" God, and they have envisaged this state as giving intense, unalloyed, and permanent satisfaction to the will and to the intellect. We know such satisfaction, to a lesser degree, in the company of those we love, in the enjoyment of great art, in the moment of solution of problems in science and mathematics, and in religious and mystical experience. The vision of God as "goodness itself", "truth itself", that which to understand is to understand everything else and which to enjoy is to make all other enjoyment insignificant, the ultimate satisfaction of intellect and will,[37] is a state of which we have a remote conception through the satisfaction of desire and intellect to which we are all used to a greater or lesser extent. In this sense, one might say, God's "goodness" is that in virtue of which he is supposed to be infinitely enjoyable; this kind of goodness is not what one would normally think of as moral goodness. One might almost say that Job, in his sufferings, asked a moral question, and got an aesthetic answer. He asked that some reason should be given why he had suffered, but was so overwhelmed with awe and the compulsion to worship by the theophany described at the end of the book[38] that he no longer felt inclined to complain.

Theists have hoped, in accordance with the promises of Jesus, that in future the hungry would be filled, and the mourners comforted.[39] To deem that God is "good" in this sense, that he will bring it about that the injustices of the present world are righted, is to regard him as good in a sense closer to that which would generally be called moral. I agree with most modern theologians, against most of them in patristic, medieval, and reformation times, that the eternal damnation of the large majority of mankind would not be consistent with God's goodness in this sense. It might be questioned whether the damnation of only a few persons, or even any one person, for eternity, would be consistent with it. It has been suggested that the teaching of the New Testament does not constrain the Christian to believe that "hell", in the sense of an unhappy state beyond this life, will last for ever;[40] but at least the eternity of hell, as well as of heaven, has usually been reckoned to be implied by it.

But whatever be the case about the everlastingness of hell, most Christian theists have believed that God makes a real offer of salvation to all men, and that no one can forfeit it except by his own fault. The views held by some Christians, notably Calvin,[41] amount in effect to a denial of this; but it is *de fide* for Catholics, and believed as a matter of course by the majority of Protestants. The goodness of God in this sense might be described as his fairness.

Theists have not usually believed that appalling evils do not happen, but only that God can and will in some way direct these to ultimate good; that they will in fact contribute to the bringing about of the new world of justice and happiness in which all the redeemed will share; that even the most agonizing things that happen tend, if we respond rightly to them, to bring us in the end to that state of total delight and fulfilment which is the vision of God. As Karl Barth has suggested, the world that God the Creator saw was good was the world redeemed in Christ,[42] that is, with its miseries removed and its potentialities for happiness realized by a principle even now at work in the world, which will come to its full fruition only in the future. The atheist does not characteristically believe in a future state for man as envisaged by Christians, Muslims, or (in a somewhat different way) Hindus. I agree that, apart from the assumption of such a future state in which present injustices and miseries are supposed to be righted, it would be very odd to claim that God the creator was good in the sense of morally good. And atheists may reasonably urge that, even granted the existence of such a future state, much suffering is so monstrous and wholly pointless that no future state for the sufferer could absolve the creator from moral turpitude as having at worst inflicted it, at best permitted it.

Two strands of thought on God's relation to evil may be disentangled from the Bible, according to one of which God is wholly opposed to evil, according to the other of which he uses it for his creative and redemptive purposes.[43] God is occasionally explicitly stated to bring about evil (Amos 3.6; Lam. 3.38), and Satan is once actually represented as an agent of the divine will (Job 1–2). Again, God is said to use the wickedness of the Assyrians and Chaldeans to punish his people. But the divine abhorrence of evil is expressed quite as plainly and even more frequently by the Old Testament writers (Isa. 43; Deut. 12.25, Ps. 94.2). In the New Testament sin and suffering are also represented as at once the enemy of God and man and able to be used ultimately for God's loving purposes. This applies especially to the supremely redemptive event of Christ's crucifixion; the treachery of Judas, the cowardice of Pilate, the cruelty of the Jewish crowd and the Roman soldiers, are all regarded as instrumental in the act of God the Father offering up his Son for the sins of the world. Thus one may summarize the doctrine of the Bible as a whole on this subject as follows: God forbids evil, but does not prevent it from occurring, and when it does so he uses it for his providential purposes.

A modern view of God, which saves his sanctity by limiting his omnipotence and also by confining the scope of his creativity, is that of A. N. Whitehead. In an important passage in *Science and the Modern World*,[44] Whitehead explicitly says that he is led to his own conception of God, which he feels to do justice to the religious experience of mankind, by the intractability on the traditional view of the problem of evil. Whitehead's doctrine of God is somewhat obscure and difficult, but its importance is being increasingly realized; I shall summarize it in greater detail at the end of this book. For Whitehead, there is a principle of creativity existing over against God, which is the foundation of possibility for all the things and events of which the world consists. God directs, influences, and limits the ongoing course of events in such a way as to enhance the good and ensure the self-destructiveness of the evil; as the "principle of concretion", he selects those events which actually occur from the indefinitely large range of possibilities.[45] Whitehead's God is not the creator in the traditional sense; the evil that there is is due to those principles underlying the cosmic process which are independent of him. But he does limit evil, and bring about its ultimate self-destruction.[46] Whitehead's God, it might be claimed, *is* in a sense a creator, because without his forming and ordering influence imposed on the chaos of possibilities there would be no "world" in the proper sense.[47] But he has not the absolute disposal of his materials implicit in the traditional notion that God creates the world out of nothing—i.e., is himself wholly responsible both for the existence and for the nature of these materials. As Barbour neatly summarizes it, Whitehead's account, with those derivative from it, "defends God's influence in the world, but not his absolute sovereignty".[48]

On the particular question of moral evil it has been claimed that it would have been possible for an omnipotent being to create agents who, although they were *free* to fall into sin, never *in fact* did so. This has been argued by Mackie, who writes: "If there is no logical impossibility in a man choosing the good on one, or on several, occasions, there cannot be a logical impossibility in his freely choosing the good on every occasion";[49] and omnipotence is only restricted by the bounds of the logically possible. More recently, Alvin Plantinga has argued that Mackie's claim that God could have created men really free to sin, while in fact ensuring that they never did so, is at bottom incoherent. God may bring it about that a man has red hair, or that he is over six feet high at the age of fourteen, or indeed that he is free to perform or not to perform a particular action A. But if God also brings it about that the man performs the action, then it cannot be said that the man is really free with respect to it. If whether the action is performed or not is entirely up to God, the agent cannot be said to be free in the matter; but if God leaves things such that whether the action is performed or not is entirely up to the agent, he cannot at the same time, as a matter of logic, ensure that it is performed.[50]

Hick admits the validity of Mackie's claim as far as it goes, but argues that a crucial difference is made if God is envisaged as creating men for a free and responsible relationship with himself. "Is it logically possible for God so to make men that they will freely respond to himself in love and trust and faith? I believe that the answer is no."[51] In effect, Hick's theodicy is based on the claim that God is concerned to bring into existence what I have termed third-type good, and that he brings about or at least permits evils of the first and second types as a logically necessary means to this; and furthermore, that the end really is worth the means. The value-judgement that is implicitly being invoked here is that one who has attained to goodness by meeting and eventually mastering temptations, and thus by rightly making responsible choices in concrete situations, is good in a richer and more valuable sense than would be one created *ab initio* in a state either of innocence or of virtue.[52] Hick adopts from some of the early Greek Fathers the theory that man was created rather innocent and immature than positively good, and he blames St Augustine, and the very large number of Christian theologians who have followed him, for claiming man to have been created so full of positive goodness and virtue that his fall into sin is wholly incomprehensible. He himself assigns a positive role to sin and evil in the providence of God, that of bringing man to a maturity and richness of moral development that could come about only as a result of a real conflict with and ultimate conquest of evil. As a Christian theologian he argues, not implausibly, that this conception does justice to the polarity of the biblical teaching on the subject.

Hick explains the existence of the animals inferior to man, and the pain which seems inseparable from their existence, as part of the whole context that it is necessary for man to exist in if he is to come to a full and responsible relationship with God. It has occasionally been suggested that there is no pain among animals; but there is so much continuity between human structure and behaviour on the one hand and that of at least the higher animals on the other as to make this view highly implausible. The lower vertebrates and invertebrates, certainly, must be capable of pain to a very much lesser degree; some insects will go on performing very complicated operations when they are being severely mutilated. This, however, does not provide adequate grounds for asserting that they feel no pain whatever on other occasions. But in the case of the lower vertebrates and invertebrates it does seem that such pain as there is is intrinsic to the process by which organic life is able to survive, by the operation of a nervous system which steers individuals away from danger. And even in the case of the higher animals the theist may properly urge that it is possible to exaggerate the quantity and degree of pain suffered, since the real atrocity of misery in men is so largely due to their capacity to be hurt by the sufferings of others, and to anticipate, remember, and brood on their own.[53]

The theist may also claim, as traditional Christians have in fact done, following some hints in the Bible,[54] that what I have called type-two evil exists on a cosmic scale owing to the "fall of the angels"; and that this has made the suffering in animal nature worse than it would otherwise have been. It may be objected that appeal to the existence of angels only adds to the problem by invoking the more obscure to shed light on the obscure. But I think this objection would be mistaken. If human beings are radically free, there is no doubt that they have sometimes acted in such a way as to increase the amount of suffering in the world.

Some suffering at least is due to the fact that human beings have abused their freedom; those who believe in angels may claim that some suffering which is not attributable to human abuse of freedom may yet be accounted for in a strictly analogous way. If angels exist, and if some of them have abused their freedom in the way that men may be said to do, then such evil as there is in the cosmos which seems over and above what God would bring to pass were he both omnipotent and wholly good, but which cannot plausibly be attributed to men, may be claimed to be due to them. Moreover, the existence of angels cannot be said to be merely a desperate hypothesis to save theism, since traditional theists have characteristically believed in angels whether they were perplexed by the problem of evil or not. On the contrary, the bearing of the existence of angels on the problem of evil suggests that to jettison the belief in angels which has characterized traditional theism, however much this may have been done by modern theists, is really to give rise to at least as many problems as are solved. The relevance of the fall of the angels to the solution of the problem of evil depends, of course, on the logical possibility of that kind of radical freedom which I discussed in the previous chapter.

It is time to summarize the difficulties presented by the problem of evil for theists, and the proffered solutions to them. God may be held to be both omnipotent and supremely good on the assumption of a future consummation, or without such an assumption. Without such an assumption, certainly, God can be called "supremely good" only on a very metaphysical and non-moral understanding of the meaning of the word "good" in this context. God's "goodness" in this sense would seem to be indistinguishable from his eternity and supreme power. Malcolm has suggested that, as a plate which is strong and resistant to wear and tear is *ipso facto* better than a plate which is identical with it in all other respects, but more fragile, so God, who as eternal is not subject to wear and tear at all, is infinitely good in this sense.[55] Rather similar is Augustine's suggestion, that "goodness" in spiritual beings is to be identified with greatness.[56] But "goodness" in this sense, which one might call "metaphysical excellence", is very different from moral goodness.

But those who claim that there exists a God who is both omnipotent and wholly good usually take into account expectation of a future life, in which the sufferers will be comforted, and the injustices of the present life ironed out. To this it may be objected:

(*a*) That such expectation is logically incoherent. This objection will be considered in chapter 6.

(*b*) That such expectation, even if it makes sense, is based upon no adequate grounds. Theists characteristically claim that God has made promises to men, corroborating these with signs; what is involved in this claim will be discussed in chapter 4.

(*c*) That even given the truth of the expectation, God could not be wholly good when he has brought into being all the evil with which his creation is infested. But given that some creatures have real freedom, that is to say, a real possibility of acting in ways other than those in which in fact they act, then God is not directly responsible for all the evil that exists. The question whether such freedom is possible was discussed in chapter 2. And if, as theists have characteristically believed, there have been free agents who have rebelled against God on a cosmic as well as on a merely terrestrial scale, at least some of the evil not attributable to human agency may similarly be removed from God's direct responsibility.[57]

(*d*) That even given the truth of the expectation, and real freedom in some creatures, God cannot be wholly good when he has *allowed* all the evil that there is in the world. (To admit that there existed anything which he neither brought into being nor allowed would be, of course, to deny his omnipotence.) To this objection, it may be replied that only in the context of a universe with the general features which this one has including its evil, is it logically possible for there to be morally good men; and therefore that, given that God wished that such creatures should exist, it was necessary for him to create a universe such as this.[58] It may still be objected that the production of such beings is not worth the evil involved; but it is difficult to see how the argument could proceed from this point, since the types of value involved seem incommensurable. One man will have a conviction that the end is not worth the means, another that it is so; and perhaps rational discussion will not do much to decide the issue.

Faced with the problem of evil, the theist may either resort to analysis of God's goodness in terms of what I have called his metaphysical excellence; or give up the doctrine of God's omnipotence or absolute goodness or both; or he may urge, in the manner of Hick, that in the special case of the creation of mature free moral agents, even the omnipotent must use evil as a means to bring about a good end. The first way may seem to the atheist an evasion, the second a capitulation, and the third at best subject to considerable difficulty. But, as Hick remarks, theology is not alone in suggesting to the philosopher problems that are a great deal easier to formulate than to resolve.[59]

4 MIRACLES

"A miracle is a violation of the laws of nature; and, as a firm and unalterable experience has established these laws, the proof against a miracle, from the very nature of the fact, is as entire as any argument from experience can possibly be imagined."[1] Thus Hume sums up the central argument of the famous section on miracles in the first *Enquiry*. According to Hume, it is intrinsic to our reasoning about matters of fact that we should regard alleged events as more or less probable in proportion to their conformity with or difference from our experience. If an event of type A has, in sixty per cent of the cases of which we have had experience, been followed by an event of type B, we regard it as fairly probable that, when an event of type A occurs again, one of type B will duly follow. When this has happened in ninety-five per cent of the observed cases, we regard it as highly probable. Since a law of nature is a conjunction of events which has *always* obtained, in a hundred per cent of the observed cases, it is, by the very nature of "probability", as improbable as possible that any miracle, or violation of such a law, has occurred. We only rely on human testimony in making such a claim; but the veracity of human testimony is by no means a law of nature, since we know by experience of any number of cases in which people lie or are deceived—especially when, as is so often the case in reports of miracles, the witnesses stand greatly to gain if people believe the tales they relate. As a matter of fact, no testimony to the occurrence of a miracle ever amounted to a proof; and even if it had, the proof would be opposed by another at least equally strong—that the law of nature allegedly violated had held in this case as in every other. Only experience gives authority, and that by no means very strong, to human testimony; and experience gives as strong support as can possibly be to the invariable operation of the laws of nature of which miracles are infringements.

A rather different, though related, objection to the claim that miracles have happened may be appended to Hume's argument. Suppose that we mean by "laws of nature" those regularities discovered in the course of events as science advances. Then what seem to be laws of nature today may very well seem not to be so a few years hence, let alone in the indefinite future. The explosion of an atomic bomb is a miracle, in the sense of an infringement of the laws of nature, in terms of nineteenth-century physics, but not in the light of knowledge which scientists have now. Therefore, however well-attested the occurrence of an event which is miraculous in the sense that it transgresses the laws of nature as these are known today, it is always possible that the event will turn out not to have been miraculous at all in the light of knowledge arrived at in future.[2] While Hume tried to show that there can never in the nature of the case be enough evidence to prove that a miracle has taken place, the conclusion of this argument is that, whatever event takes place, we are never in a proper position to state confidently that it is miraculous.

Consideration of this argument readily suggests an objection which applies to Hume's as well: in both cases, it may be felt, the proffered definition of "miracle" is somewhat inept. In order to deal properly with the concept of miracle as employed by traditional theists, it is necessary to find a definition which takes account of actual alleged examples. Let us take those attributed (whether truly or falsely is not now at issue) to Jesus in the four Gospels. These have two distinguishing characteristics: (*a*) they are events which are striking and out of the ordinary; (*b*) they are symbolic representations of the relation between God and man which Christians claim to have been shown by and through the life of Jesus.

Now Augustine proposed a definition of miracle which perfectly fits these paradigm cases in the Gospels. When God acts in his usual manner, he suggested, we call the result nature; when he brings about striking or unusual events for the instruction and admonition of men, we call them miracles.[3] (The story of the coin in the fish's mouth[4] is a possible solitary exception in the canonical Gospels, in that it seems to be without theological significance; the "apocryphal Gospels", later collections of downright fictional material about Jesus, are full of such examples.)

It is brought out particularly by the Fourth Gospel, though indeed scarcely less by the other three when attentively read, that the miracles attributed to Jesus are not just demonstrations of power to draw attention to his status and to the importance of what he was saying; they are themselves expressive of who he was and what he was doing for mankind. He is the bringer of new life and symbolizes the fact in the raising of Lazarus; he is the bread without which men starve in their spiritual life and shows it in the feeding of the five thousand; he it is who enlightens mankind, as is brought out in the context of the cure of the man born blind.[5] Christ conquers the fury of internal passion and external danger for believers as he stilled the raging of the sea, changes the water of their religious ritual into the wine of his symbolized presence, expels their demons of hatred and selfishness as he did the demons of mental illness, and fills them with his risen life as he did the hungry multitude with food.[6] It is important here that it is not at all a question of understanding an acrostic or cypher, of which the sign can be dispensed with once the interpretation is found; the symbols of divine power continue to convey and express meaning in a way that a mere accurate description of what is being done cannot do. The difference between the discerning of the meaning of such symbols and the solution of a puzzle is like the difference between a kiss as the expression of love and shouting and abuse as the expression of anger on the one hand, and the mere statement that one loves or is angry on the other; or the difference between a list of propositions about the emotional problems of old men on the one hand, and *King Lear* as expressive of the tragedy of old age on the other.

Every religious community identifies itself and expresses its attitude to the whole of life by means of and by reference to a set of stories, its "mythology". These stories are characteristically about the adventures and mutual relationships of divine or semi-divine beings. In much the same way as the Greeks with their pantheon and the Norsemen with theirs, Christians see the difficulties and achievements of life in terms of the story of Jesus, particularly of his death and resurrection, which they thus regard as the "Word of God" *par excellence.* Christians are men who die and rise *with* Christ, who live and strive *in* Christ, and who thus associate themselves with him by reciting the story about him (the ministry of the Word) and by the performance of commemorative rites (the Sacraments); for it is by this active and committed remembrance of the story and the allowing of it to permeate the whole living of their lives that the gracious power of God is held pre-eminently to be bestowed on believers. Now it is characteristic of the stories by means of which religious communities, whether

Christian or otherwise, identify themselves, that some of the events which they describe are contrary to the normal course of nature. It is such events, which are not only of symbolic power in the lives of men (as other events of such stories are), but are also out of the ordinary *as* events, which are strictly speaking miracles. Thus the nature of miracles, as of the religious stories of which accounts of them form a part, is radically misunderstood if they are not seen in relation to the life of the religious communities in which they are significant.

That such stories have the compelling power in human life that I have described cannot be doubted; the question of *how* they do so is however a difficult and disputed one. The theory that the great religions simply pander to human wishes, and that respect for their characteristic stories derives from this, does not seem to me to fit the known facts.[7] In fact the psychological mechanisms by which these stories and the rites which accompany them have the power in human life that they do has been described exhaustively, and fairly plausibly to my mind, by C. G. Jung.[8] Now, according to Aquinas, who is only making clear what is implicit in the Bible, God speaks to men by means of events rather as men speak to one another by means of words.[9] The researches of Jung and others, which multiply the many obvious analogies between the events related by the biblical authors and other religious stories, suggest that, if God does this, he uses a natural language of signs which functions independently of the context of the Christian revelation. Parallels can be found to the central doctrines and rites of the Christian religion at times and in places where there is no possibility of mutual influence. Crosses with victims on them were to be found in primitive America before the arrival of Europeans; the Aztec maize god was partaken of by his votaries in the form of bread.

The fact of these correspondences is not disputable; the only serious question is how they are to be accounted for. The traditional Christian believer can claim that, in this one case of the crucifixion and resurrection of Jesus Christ, the myth of the dying and rising god, which occurs in so many cultures, has actually taken place; God has here provided a historical key, so to speak, for a lock ready made, or providentially prepared, in human religious psychology. An alternative explanation, which would be upheld either by an unbeliever or by the kind of believer whose faith is a vision of life without historical or eschatological truth-conditions, is that the Gospel story is a synthesis of various mythological themes, of tremendous value perhaps as such, but with no very close relation to history. This point of view is well expressed by Jung:

At a very early stage . . . the real Christ vanished behind the emotions and projections that swarmed about him far and near; immediately and almost without trace he was absorbed into the surrounding religions and moulded into their archetypal exponent. . . . The most important of the symbolical statements about Christ are those which reveal the attributes of the hero's life [in other words, what he shares with other cult-heroes] —improbable origin, divine father, hazardous birth, rescue in the nick of time, precocious development, conquest of the mother and of death, miraculous deeds, a tragic, early and symbolically significant manner of death, post-mortem effects (re-appearances, signs and marvels, etc.).[10]

There are at least two distinct questions, corresponding to the two aspects of a miracle which I have described, which have to be asked in relation to any miracle-story: (*a*) How is it significant for the members of the religious community within which the story is told? (*b*) Did the event, or at least something very like it as described in the story, actually happen? It is of course possible to admit that such a story as that told in the Old Testament of the prophet Jonah is highly unlikely to be historically true, while appreciating to the full the graphic and telling manner in which it conveys certain aspects of human destiny. To go on harping, whether with credulity or with contempt, on the question whether Jonah was really swallowed and later vomited out alive, is to miss the point of the story; which can evidently be understood by anyone who has shirked his duty or evaded his responsibility, and has been unceremoniously forced back to it by sheer pressure of circumstances. But the story of Jesus Christ, including its miraculous element, cannot be dealt with as only significant in this kind of way, if the attitude to it of traditional Christian theists is to be rightly understood. The symbolic power or "profound truth" of the story of this life is beyond question; but so is that of countless other religious stories, like those of the Greek or the Norse gods, or *a fortiori* those current in still-living religions such as Hinduism and Buddhism. The literal truth of a Christianity, as opposed to its mere profound truth as an illustration of the glory and tragedy of human life, depends on the historical truth (at least in the main) of these stories, and on the truth of the eschatological beliefs of which the mighty acts which Jesus Christ has already performed are the ground.

The question of the historicity of the miracle-stories in the Gospels is thus entwined in the larger question of what is at stake in general in Christian belief—whether it is exclusively experience of new life or "authentic existence" here and now, or whether it is also, and even more centrally, beliefs about the past and the future which cannot be exclusively verified in present experience. Thus the question of whether the miracles actually happened or did not happen cannot be set aside as of no real moment to the Christian theist. From the point of view of their exceptional nature as events, the miracles of Jesus may be divided into three main types: (*a*) those healing miracles which present no special difficulty of credence to those who are familiar with hypnotism and other psychological phenomena.[11] In this class are to be included the cures of demoniacs, of the crippled man at the pool of Bethesda, and of the man with a withered hand.[12] (*b*) those for which this kind of explanation is much less plausible. Among these are the healings of paralytics, of the blind, of the deaf, and of lepers.[13] Also to be included here, as extreme cases, are raisings of the dead, like that of the daughter of Jairus, the widow of Nain's son, and Lazarus. (*c*) those in which power over the forces of nature, and not only over man, is displayed. Examples are the blasting of the fig-tree, the stilling of the storm, the walking on the sea, the feedings of the four thousand and five thousand, and the changing of water into wine.[14]

Several possibilities may be considered. The first is that none of these events occurred at all. A Christian exegete of the school of Bultmann would be quite content with this conclusion. The essence of the Christian message, he would say, is the availability for man here and now of the authentic existence conferred by God's judgment and forgiveness. The miracle-stories of the Gospel were evolved by the primitive Christian preachers, according to this view, to convey this message to their hearers, and they may still do so to us, though we should recognize their historical falsity. But on the traditional account, the miracles of Jesus are not only signs of the possibility of new life for the Christian here and now; they are also signs *and evidence* of Christ's special status and authority to proclaim a state of affairs which is only to be brought into being in the future. It is thus no coincidence that many of those theologians who have regarded the traditional historical claims about Jesus as indifferent have regarded the traditional eschatological claims as also indifferent. In so far as authentic existence or religious experience in the present are all that is at stake in Christian belief, the historical truth or falsity of the miracle-stories about Jesus, so long as their recital conveys such authentic existence or religious experience, is evidently of no importance. But in so far as the mighty acts of Jesus in the past are signs and evidence of his authority to proclaim that the future of man will turn out in a particular way, it must be important that he performed at the very least some of the mighty acts ascribed to him.

It has been pointed out that other stories with a historical basis have been elaborated in the course of transmission with accounts of wonders not wholly dissimilar to those in the Gospels. On the other side it has been urged that the time which elapsed between the events which the Gospels describe and the writing of the Gospels was not long enough, particularly if the cultural milieu of transmission in this case is taken into account, for any very extensive elaboration to have taken place. Also the accounts of miracles appear to be rather an organic element in the Gospel narrative than readily detachable from the rest. It may indeed be more consistent with historical probability to hold that the Gospels are almost entirely mythical than that one may at once rely on the substantial historicity of the non-miraculous elements and not rely on that of the miraculous.

A second possibility to be considered is that a fair proportion of those "miracles" which can be explained plausibly in psychological terms actually occurred and that the rest did not. On this hypothesis one would expect a critical sifting of the Gospels to differentiate miracles of the first class distinguished above as among the more primitive material and those of the other two as comparatively secondary. So far as I can see, it does not do so, according to present knowledge, except when, as often happens, the critic allows his evaluation of the intrinsic probability of the events described to determine which part of the material is primary, which secondary.

Thirdly, it might be argued that 'miracles' of all three kinds were wrought by Jesus, but that, even if they are not now susceptible to explanation in terms of scientific laws, they will be at some time in the future. But, as I have tried to show, someone who argued in this way, if he claimed to be proving by it that miracles have never taken place, would be using the word "miracle" in an unusual or misleading sense, deriving rather from an account like Hume's than from what is in fact at issue in the traditional belief of Christian theists. At the very least, if Jesus performed the acts attributed to him by the Gospels, that would constitute all the basis there could well be for saying that he had unusual powers. Whether these powers turn out ultimately to be explicable in terms of laws which are in some sense natural does not seem really to affect their status as miracles. At all events, such acts, if they occurred, stood out from the normal run of actions, and make sense as symbolic of God's ultimate purposes for men; this is enough to constitute them as miracles in the traditional sense.

An account of miracle which well represents the point of view of radical modern Protestant exegesis is presented by R. H. Fuller.[15] Fuller says that our modern concepts of "nature" and the "natural" are alien to the thought of the Bible, which therefore provides no basis for the conception of a miracle as an event contrary to nature. A miracle in the biblical sense is rather a theologically significant event or course of events. The deliverance of Israel from Egypt was the pre-eminent example of such a "miracle" for the Old Testament, and the life and work of Jesus Christ, culminating in the Crucifixion and Resurrection, for the New. These major miracles were each accompanied by minor miracles, such as the ten plagues of Egypt and the cures and exorcisms wrought by Jesus. Israel's cultus, and the preaching of the Word and celebration of the sacraments in the Christian Church, are also, as Fuller sees it, "miracles" in the biblical sense (theologically significant events); but not in their own right, only as making present and effective for believers the supreme miracles of the Exodus and the Incarnation.[16]

Fuller's usage seems to me to alter the usual significance of the term "miracle" in a way that is unnecessary and misleading. Certainly, on the biblical account, many events are theologically significant without being in any way abnormal; such events may usefully be termed "sign-events". It corresponds more with ordinary usage to reserve the term "miracle" for those sign-events which are strikingly abnormal *as* events. As Fuller admits, the sign-events which are the matter of the biblical narrative are often abnormal in this way, though not always so;[17] and surely such abnormal events are in an important sense "contrary to nature", if by "nature" one means "the normal course of events". Thus Fuller's observation that the Bible has no term corresponding to "nature", does not enable us to answer the question whether, to make explicit what is implicit in the biblical account, we ourselves may have to use the term, or at least one more or less identical with it in meaning. We may now express Fuller's point as follows: the Exodus for the Old Testament Israelites, and the life and work of Jesus Christ for the Church, are crucial sign-events, made present to and effective for believers by the subsidiary sign-events of the cult. The major sign-events are accompanied and set in high relief by minor sign-events, only some of which have that striking and paranormal quality which marks them out as miracles strictly speaking. For example, the cleansing of the temple, and the triumphal entry into Jerusalem, are acts of Jesus which are sign-events without being miracles.[18]

Fuller's account in fact has exactly the opposite disadvantage to Hume's; it concentrates exclusively on the symbolical, at the expense of the exceptional and striking aspects, of an event, which constitute it as a miracle in the traditional Christian sense. The Crucifixion is the most obvious example of an event supremely significant for Christians, which is yet not miraculous in the usual sense. One might say, adapting an expression from the New Testament itself, that miracles are "signs and wonders";[19] but that while the Crucifixion is certainly a "sign" it is not a "wonder"; while God speaks to men through it, it is not a striking exception in itself to the normal course of events. There would have been nothing astonishing, to a spectator of the time, in a man being crucified, in the way there would have been in his walking on the water or rising from the dead. A miracle in the strict sense, though, is both a sign and a wonder.

Now this account of what a miracle is fits actually alleged cases and does not drag in the tiresome and elusive concept of a "law of nature". When people want to know whether witches exist they generally want to know whether there are women who fly on broomsticks, or have sexual intercourse with the devil in the form of a black cat, or exert malign influences on people by the chanting of spells and the brewing of potions; they do not just wish to know whether there are hysterical women with a certain range of symptoms. Similarly, when people want to know whether miracles happen or ever have happened, they want to know whether there have occurred events similar to those described in the Gospels; they are not really interested in whether such events, if they happened, infringed something so obscure and recondite as a "law of nature". Thus such arguments against the occurrence of miracles as Hume's and Nowell-Smith's depend on a conception of "miracle" which does not really fit the paradigm cases. To say that all the odd events described in the Gospels happened, but that they occurred somehow in accordance with scientific laws and not as exceptions to them, would not really be to contradict the historical claims of traditional Christians. Not that it is necessarily wrong to say that miracles are in fact exceptions to "laws of nature" in some sense; what is unfortunate is to define a miracle in this way. If modern physicists are right that such laws of nature as science progressively discovers are based on the random behaviour of huge numbers of fundamental particles, it is only to be expected that there will very occasionally be exceptions to such laws. It may be that, if events like those described in the Gospels actually took place, they did so in this way. But their status as such exceptions is not intrinsic to their essence as miracles.

The question about miracles which is of importance for traditional Christians is whether the marvellous events alleged in the Gospels, or at least events very like them, actually took place. There are many apparent short cuts to answering this question, none of them satisfactory. An unbeliever may argue, in the manner of Hume, that since other accounts such as these, if they occurred in a merely secular context, would be rejected out of hand, the same treatment ought to be accorded to these accounts themselves. The believer may retort that, since this piece of history is *ex hypothesi* unique, the normal canons of historical inquiry cannot be applied to it. Both arguments are open to attack. The fact is, surely, that in the case of any alleged historical event or series of events which is unique in kind, some of the normal canons of historical inquiry will apply, others not. For instance, the claim that since all other stories of wonder-workers turn out on close examination, whenever such examination is feasible, to be false, this story must be false as well, will not do (even if its premise is true, which it is probably not), because of the uniqueness of the case as alleged. However, in as far as the Gospel narrative as a whole appears more and more like acknowledged myths and legends, and less and less like acknowledged records of historical events—when the cultural background of the stories, their method of transmission, and the length of time between the alleged events and the composition of the documents describing them, are all taken into account—it becomes correspondingly more irrational to believe in its historicity and consequently to believe in the Christian faith in its traditional sense. The most competent scholars are still very much divided on this verdict, but there is no reason why this state of affairs should always be so.[20]

It has often been held by traditional theists that miracles, if they take place, are not only signs of God's purposes for those who already believe in him, but also evidence for the existence and nature of God which ought to convince unbelievers. Many recent theists, however, have opposed this claim.[21] It may be argued that miracles can never be evidence for God's existence or his activity, since the sceptic can always object to any alleged instance either that the event did not happen as reported, or that, if it did so, it took place according to the normal course of nature, though through a causal process which scientists have not yet managed to unravel. In order to examine this contention properly it seems useful to deal with it in the context of a particular kind of case, the miraculous cure of disease. (This category includes not only most of the examples in the Gospels, but also the most well-known and well-documented series in the history of modern Europe, those performed at Lourdes.) It might be said that all cases of this kind which impartial investigation cannot invalidate as due to delusion or fabrication can be explained in terms of psychiatric laws, according to the same pattern as cures of the more bizarre types of neurotic disorder such as hysterical paralysis. But investigation of psychotherapeutic cures so far strongly suggests that actual organic deterioration is never immediately arrested, let alone counteracted.[22] Now suppose both that the evidence for an alleged miracle were to stand up to investigation, and also that the cure involved instantaneous restoration of organic tissue. The laws of psychotherapy, so far as they are known from other cases, exclude the possibility of this event. If the sceptic says that they will later be found to account for it, he will be indulging in a sheer act of faith, since the present developments of the science of psychotherapy show no sign whatever that they will do so. If he claims that to accept the event as a miracle is to abandon any attempt at rational explanation, this again will not do; since to call an event a miracle is to explain it, after a fashion, by describing it as a mighty act of God to reassure his people that he will ultimately bring to full fruition his gracious promises to them. If the sceptic can provide even a sketch of an alternative explanation, well and good; the believer may well encourage him to do so, since he need not be inclined to deny that many reports of miracles have been false, and, unless his own faith is very shaky, will be as keen as the sceptic to detect credulity and imposture.

It is always possible, of course, as Nowell-Smith suggests, that those miracles which are comparatively well-attested will be seen to be in some sense normal in the course of future scientific discovery; but it is at least equally possible that some miracles will both continue to resist such interpretation and also be attested in such a way as to stand up to the most rigorous investigation. In as far as it is true of any alleged event that (*a*) the evidence for it stands up to impartial scrutiny, (*b*) explanation in terms of scientific laws suggests and goes on suggesting that it could not have happened as part of the normal course of events, and (*c*) at the same time it is not completely "arbitrary", in that it stands with other similar events as significant of the alleged promises of God—it is reasonable to claim in a particular instance that a miracle has occurred.

It will be observed that the question of whether, and if so in what sense, an event is arbitrary, arises in connection with miracles as well as free actions. The argument against the occurrence of miracles, like that against the occurrence of radically free actions, will appear stronger than it is if it is assumed that they must by definition be absolutely arbitrary, or resistant to all explanation whatever. They may be so in one sense, if they resist and continue to resist explanation in terms of normal events. But they are not so in another sense, as forming part of a language of symbolic events through which God is supposed to communicate with man.

I have not tried to argue here that miracles have in fact ever taken place. I have simply tried to show that if there are events which are both well-attested and also significant in the kind of way I have described, and moreover resist and continue to resist explanation in terms of laws governing normal events, then such "miraculous" events may properly form part of an apologetic for certain kinds of theism. Such "miracles", if they were to occur, would not exactly prove the existence of God to the honest secularist investigator; they would, however, be a constant reminder to him that there was some factor which he had not taken into account. The sceptic may properly try to demonstrate, in relation to the more impressive cases, that such "miracles" do not and have not occurred (he may, for example, impugn in detail the evidence for, or construct naturalistic explanations of, the more notable cases at Lourdes); but, if my arguments here have been at all correct, he had better abandon the claim that the concept of a miracle is incoherent.

In as far as a well-attested event resists and continues to resist explanations of a scientific kind, it seems that it may be claimed to be against the "laws of nature" in something like the sense intended by Hume. But even if it is held that there are or have been no such events in fact, a real event may still be held to be a miracle in a sense quite close to the traditional one, if it is both significant and stands out from the normal run of events in such a way as to compel attention. An example of this kind of event has been given in an article by R. F. Holland.[23] A small child wanders onto a railway line along which an express train is due to pass. The express train is running on time as it approaches the child, and there is a bend in the line so that the driver cannot possibly see the child in time to stop the train. And yet the train does in fact stop within a few feet of the child. The driver had fainted owing to the movement of a clot of blood, and the train had stopped through the action of a safety-device when his hand ceased to exert pressure on the control lever. Here there is no question of the breaking of any law of nature; the event is striking as a coincidence. Yet it would perhaps not be unreasonable for the mother of the child to claim that a miracle had occurred; in that something had happened, against all the probabilities given the antecedent conditions, which was of immense significance for her life. It is certainly a "miracle" in the minimal sense suggested by the above reference to St Augustine, in that it is an event which both stands out as remarkable in itself, and may steadily be understood as significant of the kind of mercy towards men which has traditionally been attributed to God by Christians.

It may be easily seen that, if it is true that "laws of nature" on the macrophysical level are the result of chance on the microphysical level, then an event which was "miraculous" in that it broke what was a law of nature on the macrophysical level could yet be explained as the result of a mighty coincidence, as in Holland's example, on the microphysical. A macrophysical event may be contrary to the "laws of nature" in two ways. It may resist and continue to resist explanation in terms of macrophysical laws, but be explicable by coincidence at the microphysical level; or it may be thus contrary to the laws of nature at both levels. It may reasonably be claimed that an event of the kind described by Holland is not a miracle in quite the full traditional sense; but it seems to me that if any events occur which, as well as conforming to the other conditions which have been ascribed to miracles, continue to resist explanation on the macrophysical level, but are yet explicable by coincidence on the microphysical, it would be peculiar to deny them the title of miracle on the latter ground alone. If someone were to acknowledge that Jesus performed all the actions attributed to him in the Gospels, but still asserted that "miracles" had not occurred since every action was explicable in terms of coincidence at the microphysical level, the implied conception of miracle would be so different from the one traditionally at issue that there would be no reason for any believer to take his objection seriously.

Of course there are many theists who do not believe in the occurrence of miracles as vindicating and illustrating God's revelation of himself, either now or in the past; but such theists ought to consider that the less difference belief in God is deemed to make to expectations about matters of fact, the more colourable is the allegation that it is a mere picture of life, aesthetically satisfying or morally useful to some, but with no claim to objective validity.

5 PRAYER

There is one common device in argument against which philosophical analysis should always be on its guard; a device which C. L. Stevenson has usefully labelled "persuasive definition".[1] Persuasive definition takes place whenever, in the course of an argument, a meaning is given to a word or phrase which is not its generally agreed one, but something that the speaker is trying to commend or attack. The device is especially common, perhaps, in political argument; "true democracy" will mean something very different to a British Conservative and a Chinese communist. Where a term has no precisely delimited meaning in general use it is a very simple matter to take advantage of the resulting ambiguities for the special purposes of a particular argument. In no part of philosophy probably is this a more recurrent danger than in the philosophy of religion. It is quite easy to show that "true" miracles occur or do not occur, that "real" prayer is efficacious or otherwise, if you deliberately frame your definitions so as to make them so. One might put it that while the section on miracles in Hume's *Enquiries* uses a persuasive definition of miracle for polemical purposes, D. Z. Phillips' *The Concept of Prayer* uses a persuasive definition of prayer for apologetic purposes. It is in order to avoid the pitfall of persuasive definition that I have tried, in analysing the concepts relevant to theistic belief, to analyse them as they are to be found in the Bible. This procedure will now be applied to the concept of prayer.

In prayer the individual and the community enjoy communion with their God.[2] In Old Testament Israel prayer presupposed the conviction that God was among his people and was acting on their behalf; his presence invited a response from them in prayer and worship and in the conduct of life in general. Prayer was offered in confidence that God would listen, a confidence sometimes so firm that thanks would be offered in anticipation of God's granting his suppliant's request.[3] But often too uncertainty on this score introduces a note of anxiety and pleading; the unhappy soul as it wrestles with God.[4] There is prayer for spiritual blessings, but still more for temporal benefits; good health, long life and prosperity are asked for, as well as the joy of participating in worship of God.[5] The Israelites prayed for the preservation of true religion, but also for the triumphant vindication of their own nation and the punishment of its enemies. There was intercession for the King and for one's countrymen.[6]

Three main types of prayer may be distinguished: petition, thanksgiving, and penitence. Petitions sometimes were accompanied by a summary of favours previously granted by God; in extreme cases this amounted to a review of Israel's history.[7] Penitential prayers typically consisted of an admission of guilt, with a request for forgiveness and for remission of punishment. Sometimes they included a plea for deliverance from danger and the promise of amendment.[8] Prayers of thanksgiving usually included an admission of man's unworthiness to receive such favours at the hands of God.[9]

The Gospels, especially that of Luke, frequently describe Jesus as in prayer.[10] He evidently prayed both publicly and privately before important acts and decisions.[11] But in virtue of his special relation with God the Father he is in the Fourth Gospel represented in effect as living in continual prayer.[12] He taught his disciples how to pray.[13] The requisites for prayer according to the New Testament view are perseverance, confidence in being heard, and absolute sincerity as opposed to external show.[14] Where prayer fulfils these conditions, its efficacy is unlimited.[15] Communal prayer is supposed to be particularly effective.[16] The prayers of the early Christians were dominated by spiritual values, though worldly blessings and trials were not left out of account.[17] Not only fellow-Christians were objects of intercessory prayer, but all men, especially those in authority, and even enemies and persecutors.[18]

The prayer of theists might be summarized as their response to God for what they believe he has done, and to what they hope he will do, on their behalf. This is why there is a close connection between prayer and doctrine; to think and feel appropriately about anything, from a scientist to a centipede, it is necessary to have some idea of what it is and what it is supposed to do or have done. Not that every layman who prays needs a knowledge of abstruse theological doctrines in order to do so; though it is probably true that even the most abstruse doctrines are ultimately deducible from what the ordinary believer must believe, at least implicitly, in order to pray properly.

In prayer the theist talks to his God; and the nature of the talk between man and God may be compared and contrasted with that between man and man. Given that God is omniscient, prayer cannot be the kind of talk which consists in giving information. Prayer is more like the kind of talk between human beings which promotes personal *rapport* between the speaker and him who is spoken to. (The sceptic might comment that God is the perfect listener, since he never answers back—just as good from this point of view if he does not exist as if he does.) Often when a man is anxious or unhappy it may make all the difference to him if he talks with another, even if he gains by it little or no information or advice. Certainly many believers when they pray obtain strength and comfort in a way analogous to this. Petitionary prayer is, of course, similar to the kind of talk which consists in asking people to do things.

It has sometimes been held, even by those who commend the the practice of prayer, that it is inevitably destroyed by philosophical reflection.[19] This claim is ambiguous. If it implies that those who reflect seriously and systematically about man's place in the universe will come to see that prayer is useless, because what efficacy it has depends only on illusion, then it could of course be combined with the commending of the practice of prayer only at the price of gross dishonesty. But it may mean only that one cannot pray to a God who is merely a philosophical abstraction, and towards whom one has no spontaneous personal feelings. I shall assume here that philosophical reflection can provide a useful critique of prayer, showing the preconceptions which underlie it and showing up for what they are those forms of it which are inconsistent with a developed understanding of man's place in the universe; but I shall not imply that prayer can be derived from philosophical reflection alone. The relationship between philsosophy and prayer might be compared to that between psychology and love. Knowledge of psychology may certainly direct and inform the spontaneous expression of love; but this does not alter the fact that it would be fatal to try to make love out of a book of psychology.

There are close connections between Christian prayer, belief, and action; though it is in a way possible to have one without the others, it is a situation as much of logical as of factual oddity. This again may be illustrated by a parallel from a non-religious context. If one man said that he believed another had conferred a very great benefit upon him, but never expressed the very slightest gratitude to the benefactor or enthusiasm about the benefit, it would be doubted whether he really believed what he claimed to believe, since the usual concomitants of such belief were so strangely lacking. In prayer a theist reflects on how it stands with him in relation to God, and therefore in relation to his own ultimate happiness; he thanks God for benefits which he has so far received, asks him for help in the future, and says he is sorry for what he has done in the past to close himself from the life-giving grace of God.

The stories in the Bible are illustrations and analogues of the various typical states of the individual believer and the believing community in relation to the grace of God. The believer articulates his understanding of his own relationship to God in terms of the classic instances provided by the mythology, legend, and history of the ancient Israelites, and more especially in terms of the characters and situations in the Gospels. (The lives of the saints provide a secondary and derivative source for Catholic and Eastern Orthodox Christians.) Every believer knows by experience his own exile in Babylon, his own cramped and filthy confinement in the belly of the fish,[20] his forty years' wanderings in the desert, and the ravaging of his country by Philistines and Assyrians. But he also knows, and goes on hoping for, mighty deliverances wrought for him by God; like the Israelites in Egypt, and in the time of the Judges, he cries out to God in his affliction, yet all the while in confident expectation that God will deliver his suppliants now as in former times.

This commemoration of particular historical events, supposed to be significant in a special way of God's gracious operation on behalf of men here and now, is, as has been shown, a central feature of prayer as the Bible presents it. The Passover commemorates the Exodus for Jews, the Eucharist the death of Jesus for Christians, by liturgical re-enactment. In commemorating these historical acts of divine deliverance, the believer expresses his eschewing of the old life turned away from God and his sharing of the new life bestowed by him.

If prayer is essentially and primarily man's response to God's gracious action on his behalf, it is clear that such constituent elements as worship, penitence, and petition should be understood in relation to this. In worship the believer expresses both adoration and fear of the giver of such gifts and the source of such power. In penitence he looks back over those past actions of his which have amounted to rebellion against God and contempt of what he offers, and resolves to do better in future. In petition he asks both in general for God's continued help of himself and others and also for particular favours. It is this petitionary element in traditional Christian prayer (which, while it does not hold an exclusive place in it, does hold a necessary and central one) that especially gives rise to philosophical difficulties.

There are two assumptions in particular which tend to give rise to reductionist accounts of prayer, or at least to descriptions of it in which this central petitionary element is missing. The first is the belief that the world order is fixed in such a way that every event is predetermined to happen just as it does happen. The second is that it is naive or even blasphemous to treat the Creator as one who is of such insignificance from the cosmic point of view as to be affected by human requests. These two beliefs are evidently inconsistent with at least one kind of petitionary prayer. This is the kind in which requests are made to God on the assumption that he may bring about certain events in a way in which he would not have done had the requests not been made, and where there is no causal connection between the events requested and any state, whether psychological or moral, which may be brought about in the individual himself by his making of the request. A prayer for the victims of an earthquake, for instance, by one who had no means either of helping them of causing them to be helped, would clearly be petitionary in the full sense which I have just suggested; whereas the prayer for courage for oneself in a dangerous situation would not be so clearly or unequivocally so. I shall refer in what follows to those prayers which conform with the definition I have given as strictly petitionary prayers.

Anyone who calls himself a Christian believer but denies that prayer can be petitionary has to answer the objection that the Lord's prayer, which was apparently commended by Jesus to his disciples as the very model of prayer, consists so largely of petitions.[21] A possible answer might be that the petitions need not be understood as strictly petitionary in the sense I have suggested.

Thus to pray for the coming of God's kingdom might be taken as simply a means of committing oneself to such moral endeavour as will tend to promote it; to pray not to be led into temptation might be understood as expressing a sense of one's moral frailty and tendency to be scared, browbeaten, or coerced into sinful behaviour; while prayer for one's daily bread might be interpreted as a salutary admission of man's dependence on his physical environment continuing to provide him with the means of life. Certainly such attitudes are closely involved in the making of these petitions as traditionally understood. And I think it might quite intelligibly be urged that the prayer as a whole, while really valuable to sophisticated and civilized people, could only be so when understood in this kind of way. But I think it would be very ignorant or dishonest to maintain either that Jesus intended the petitions to be understood only in this way, or that his disciples so understood them. I think it is quite certain that they were intended to include a strictly petitionary element.

Of course there can be no question that the primary purpose of the prayer of the Christian is that his will should be conformed to that of God, so that he should ultimately be brought to salvation, and not to ask God to make things happen in a particular way. Yet to admit that the strictly petitionary aspect of Christian prayer is not the primary one is not to concede that it is dispensable; and the fact is that Christians are quite plainly told by Jesus to pray for particular things that they want.[22] The men of the Old Testament prayed for health and wealth and material benefits; and, although the first generation of Christians may have laid greater emphasis on spiritual good, there is no sign that their attitude was fundamentally different.

Strictly petitionary prayer is sometimes stigmatized as a survival of magic.[23] But there are important distinctions to be drawn. In intercourse between man and man there is a fundamental difference between one asking another to do something (in such a way that he can refuse if he pleases) and one putting pressure on another in such a way that he has no alternative but to comply with the demands made on him. The second kind of transaction with a god or gods may properly be termed magical; where if the appropriate ritual is properly performed or the appropriate formula exactly recited by the votary, the deity is compelled to grant his request. But in the case of strictly petitionary prayer on the part of

Christian theists there is no question of, as it were, putting constraint on God. On the other hand, if strictly petitionary prayer is a valid activity it must sometimes be the case that God brings events to pass because a man has asked him to; and this must imply, presumably, that had the request not been made the event would not have come to pass. To say that all strictly petitionary prayer is magical is to imply that, whenever an agent complies with a request, it will always be the case, in the last analysis, that he has no alternative but to comply with it. This position is certainly a consequence of determinism; but I have already argued that one need not assume that *human* actions are subject to any such restriction; and this would appear to apply *a fortiori* to divine actions.[24]

The commonest argument against strictly petitionary prayer is that it must be ineffective since all events are predetermined in their causes. The apologist may deny either the premiss, or the inference, or both. He may claim, for instance, that human actions are not so predetermined, and thus that one may ask God to influence them. But if he still accepts the validity of the inference, he could hardly pray about tomorrow's weather, since such a prayer would seem to presuppose an incredible degree of indeterminacy in the events of nature—unless he were praying for nothing less than a suspension of the natural order. Similarly, to justify petitionary prayer on the basis of the indeterminacy postulated by modern physics, as William Pollard has done,[25] is to restrict its scope within a fairly narrow range. But the apologist, whether he accepted the premiss or not, might deny the inference. Petitionary prayer may be effective even in the case of events predetermined in their causes, on the ground that an omniscient God might have acted yesterday, or a thousand million years ago, with a view to what his suppliant is freely praying today. This possibility depends on an account of God's knowledge of future contingencies like that advanced by Boethius, which I discussed in the third chapter. If this conception is a valid one, it does not necessarily seem irrational to pray today about tomorrow's weather, even if one accepts that its general character, which is presumably all that is of importance for the suppliant or his community, is predetermined in weather conditions already prevalent. On this view, too, I cannot see why it should not be possible to pray about events which have already occurred, but of which one does not know the outcome.[26] If a woman knows that her husband has just taken part in a dangerous military exercise, but does not yet know the issue of it, it is not irrational, on this account of the matter, for her to go on praying for his safety.

There are, it seems, two possible ways out for the apologist for strictly petitionary prayer who is confronted by the argument that his practice is inconsistent with the scientific world view, according to which events succeed each other in accordance with regular laws. He may either draw attention to the indeterminacy of modern physics and suggest that God takes account of requests made to him in the immediate working out of events; or he may claim that, even if nature were completely deterministic, God in his omniscience would know eternally of a man's prayer at a particular time, and so might arrange events from the beginning to take account of that prayer. Of course this last argument, though independent of the doctrine of natural indeterminism, is not inconsistent with it.

Prayer has been summarized as adoring God, confessing to him, thanking him, and making requests to him.[27] To adore God is consciously to value him above all else, and to anticipate and long for the bliss and glory of the enjoyment of him. For a man to confess to God is for him to acknowledge, and so be put in the way to do something about, those elements in himself, his selfishness and unkindness and disproportionate desire for things not in the long run worthwhile, that impede him in his journey towards God. He thanks God for those things which have either given him happiness, or which according to God's promise, however distressing in themselves, are putting him in the way of ultimate bliss. These three aspects of prayer, adoring, confessing, and thanking, evidently do not involve the special difficulties raised by petitionary prayer.

If prayer is conceived of as without this strictly petitionary element, it may still be used at least for moral improvement, for the obtaining of a state of mystical rapture or detachment, or both. Kant is pre-eminent among those philosophers who have emphasized the moral element in prayer at the expense of the mystical and the strictly petitionary. In his view the object of private prayer is to establish in oneself the will to do good, that of public prayer to confirm this disposition in the community as a whole.[28] From the mystical point of view prayer is valued as a means of achieving certain psychological states, either of intense devotion or of contemplative detachment. These states may be considered not only intrinsically valuable, but also as a means of gaining serenity in face of the pains, irritations, and anxieties characteristic of ordinary life. If prayer is conceived mainly as a means to experiences of these kinds, morality is usually regarded as a subsidiary end; but sometimes it falls out of view altogether. (This seems to have been the case with some of St Paul's converts, some Gnostic sects, and some extremists at the time of the Reformation.) When either the exclusively moral or the exclusively mystical view of prayer is fully worked out, what may sometimes be seen to be at issue is not so much a relationship with God, as a goal-state of the religious life; and the postulation of some being other than man, to whom man is related in prayer, may seem unnecessary, or even intrusive. An interesting compromise is hit on by the non-dualist schools of Hinduism, which teach that the end of the soul's pilgrimage to "God" is the full realization that it is identical with him.

There is, of course, a serious question whether it is logically possible to pray without belief that there is some God or gods to whom prayer is addressed. It has been said that "belief in the personality of God is the necessary presupposition, the fundamental condition, of all prayer".[29] But the religious exercises of many non-theistic Buddhists and Hindus have so much in common with prayer as practised by theists that it is perhaps misleading to deny them the name of prayer. Yet however widely the concept of prayer is understood, it is always true of the man who prays that, by meditation and the recital of formulae, he tries to attain to a form of life which is somehow better or more fulfilled than the form of life which he enjoys here and now.

Prayer is the expression of a primitive impulsion to a higher, richer, intenser life. . . . The hungry pygmy who begs for food, the entranced mystic, absorbed in the greatness and beauty of the infinite God, the guilt-oppressed Christian who prays for forgiveness of sins and assurance of salvation—are all seeking life; they seek a confirmation and richness of their realization of life.[30]

All that is presupposed for prayer on this minimal definition is the comparative misfortune, or misery, or worthlessness of the man or community that prays and the conception of a state which is better and somehow attainable. Christ, according to St John's gospel, said that he came to bring more abundant life to men;[31] prayer, at the very least, is man's attempt to avail himself, by meditation or pleading rather than by action, of more abundant life. It need not necessarily involve the assumption that this better life will be the enjoyment of fellowship with God or the gods. The life envisaged may consist of moral improvement or mystical rapture or the betterment of one's material conditions. The after-life looked forward to by traditional Christian theists combines all these elements.

Traditional Christian prayer, of course, is definitely the enjoyment and anticipation of a personal relationship with God; it includes a mystical, a moral, and a strictly petitionary element, but none of these in an exclusive or autonomous way. In such mystical experiences as he may have, the believer regards himself as enjoying by anticipation a bliss which will be consummated in the future; he prays for power to become morally better, since moral improvement will be a sign of the effective operation of God's grace in him; and he prays for particular benefits for himself and others, in the belief (founded on the gospel) that the eternal will of God allows the particular requests of creatures a place within itself.

The life of the Christian believer as a whole is supposed to consist in a relationship with God which is inaugurated now and brought to a fulfilment of unimaginable bliss in the future. If we call the attainment of this bliss "salvation", prayer may be seen as an attempt to gain either (*a*) salvation for oneself or others, or (*b*) relative happiness or alleviation of misery for oneself or others in the present life, or (*c*) both of these. Even if strictly petitionary prayer is invalid, it may still be claimed that a man's prayer tends to promote his own relative happiness in the present, and perhaps his salvation, by helping him to bear with fortitude whatever happens to him, or empowering him to act in such a way as to improve his situation. It may promote the happiness of others, and conceivably their salvation, by enabling him to behave with more understanding, kindness, or moral probity towards them, by causing him to avoid inflicting harm, and to engage in bestowing positive good on them. But at least it seems to follow inescapably from such a conception of prayer that prayers for others cannot have any effect on them which is not brought about by the subsequent action of the man who prays. This would entail a very restricted view of the kind of prayer known as "intercession", which may consequently be said, at least as usually understood, to presuppose the validity of strictly petitionary prayer.

A peculiarity of the petitionary prayer of many theists, which gives rise to special philosophical difficulties, is that they ask not only for good fortune but also to be delivered from sin—in other words, to be made morally good. Now the Stoics argued that a man could not properly pray to God or the gods for moral goodness, and their position has some plausibility.[32] After all, if moral goodness is something which God bestows on some men and fails to bestow on others, and which it is not up to each individual man to achieve for himself, in what sense can it really *be* moral goodness? It may seem intrinsic to the concept of moral goodness that it can only be gained by an individual's own efforts. But according to the Christian conception the sanctified life, and therefore the virtuous one, is that which is lived in utter dependence on God; not in confidence in oneself, but in constant acceptance through prayer of the grace of God. One might even say that, on the Christian account of the matter, there *is* no such thing as virtue; this would follow so long as was meant by "virtue" desirable moral qualities for which an agent himself is alone responsible. It is essential to human goodness as Christians understand it that what goodness a man has is due to God, and not merely to his own unaided efforts; hence prayer is appropriate both in thanks for whatever goodness one may have been granted and as petition that God's gift of goodness may still be granted to one in the future. Either undue confidence in the present or continuing existence of one's own goodness, or the despising of others as morally inferior, is inconsistent with the Christian doctrine of our dependence on God not only for our existence but for whatever virtue we may have. The disposition to pray is merely the natural consequence of what Christians believe to be the extent of man's dependence on God.

Short of the eschatological prospect which has traditionally characterized the Christian life, prayer is bound to appear as something very different from what it seems to be in the light of it. D. Z. Phillips' interesting recent book on this subject, *The Concept of Prayer*, is a good illustration of the point. For Phillips prayer, and the whole religious context within which it occurs, is autonomous and self-justifying. The factual presuppositions intrinsic to traditional Christianity are certainly not presupposed by Phillips. On the traditional view, too, God is the agent of whose acts the world consists, and who is bringing the world and men into a certain state in future, in relation to which prayer and other religious activities are to be understood. But Phillips seems in effect to reject the belief, which it must be admitted is presupposed throughout the Bible, that God is an agent of any kind.[33] He rightly stresses that the question of what kind of existence God is supposed to have has to be settled before it can usefully be asked whether God exists;[34] and it is just on this question that his view differs radically from the traditional one. For God to exist, he seems to imply, is for certain states of profound feeling and exaltation to be available to men who pray. Now, on the traditional view, this is certainly held to be a *sign* that God exists, but much more is held to be entailed by the proposition that he exists.

Phillips complains that philosophers have made unnecessary problems for themselves by "creating a false gap between the act of praying and the God to whom prayer is addressed".[35] But one can only close this gap at the cost of conceiving God in a way radically different from that of traditional theism. (This is not to deny, of course, that considerations of philosophy or science or morality might compel religious people to abandon the traditional concept of God; the point here is just that, if they argue in a certain way, they will in effect be doing this.) For Phillips religion, including the "God" who seems to exist internally to religious activity rather as races exist in the running of them, is an aspect of human life valuable in itself and wholly self-justifying; indeed, he goes so far as to say that "the whole conception . . . of religion standing in need of justification is confused".[36] This depends, it seems to me, on what is meant by "religion". It might quite intelligibly be claimed, where the religion concerned was historical Christianity (which is not too untypical, in the relevant respects, of religion in general), that it involved false historical judgements and fostered illusory hopes, or had immoral or anti-social effects. Now in as far as it is ever claimed that these features are characteristic of religion, then presumably the rebuttal of these claims, not merely as irrelevant but as factually erroneous, will be in effect a justification of religion. Phillips holds that to believe in God is not like believing in a theory, but is synonymous with worshipping.[37] On the traditional view, belief in God certainly *includes* the disposition to worship, but includes also assent to the truth of certain theories, belief in which is not wholly unlike belief in theories of science or history.

The philosopher, he says, is guilty of a deep misunderstanding if he thinks that his task in discussing prayer is to try to determine whether contact is made with God.[38] I think he means this caution to apply to discussion of prayer in general; certainly it is easy to point to individual cases where it might properly be said that contact was not being made with God. One might describe the pharisee, as contrasted with the publican in the parable of Jesus, in some such terms as these.[39] There are sinister and pathological uses of prayer, as when people pray for those whom they are destroying by myriad pinpricks of subtle unkindness—here the function of prayer is to assure him who prays that he cannot be destroying his fellow-man, when he is so good as to pray for him! Phillips, who rightly holds that a criterion for the genuineness of prayer is its relation to the whole life of him who prays,[40] would perhaps agree that here is a case where contact is not being made with God. (He might say that such a case was not really prayer at all, rather than prayer which did not make contact with God; but this seems a question of the use of words on which there hangs little of importance.)

Phillips talks of the hope which should characterize the man of prayer as "'hope' in the sense of ability to live with oneself".[41] But the hope of traditional Christianity, which consists in the expectation of future bliss, may well make a man, in the relevant sense, *unable* to live with himself as he is now. Hope has been usefully described as a mean between despair and presumption, despair being the effective conviction that one cannot be sanctified and so brought to blissful union with God, presumption the conviction that one needs no further sanctification. Despair and presumption are both refusals to undergo the often painful change by which men can be fitted for their future life with God. It is no wonder that Aquinas associates prayer with the virtue of hope.[42]

I have been concerned in this section to emphasize the place of prayer in the religious life as a whole. I have tried to show that there is some ambiguity in the notion of "petition", but that, on any account, Christian prayer must contain some petitionary element, if it is not to become radically different from what it has been up to the present time.

6 THE SOUL AND AFTERLIFE

A catechism which used to be widely employed in the religious instruction of Catholic children exhorts them to be more concerned with looking after their souls than with looking after their bodies. This may be interpreted, in a relatively sophisticated way, to imply that it is more important for our ultimate well-being to develop our morality, our intellect or our religious life, than to diet properly or avoid taking undue physical risks. On a less sophisticated level, the suggestion seems to be that each human being consists of two more or less detachable bits, a soul and a body. Augustine defined a human being as a soul using a body; he was influenced in this by the dualism which characterized one stage of Plato's thought.[1] On this view, there is no difficulty in the idea of an afterlife, which may be conceived simply as the detachment of a man's soul or imperishable part from his body or perishable part; the only question is how the soul ever came to be associated with something so fundamentally alien to its nature as the body. Another influential conception of the soul is that of Aristotle and Aquinas, who understood the soul to be the "form" of any living thing.[2] This idea is in some ways obscure; what is important about it in comparison with the Platonic conception is that it suggests a far more intimate relation between the soul and the body; in this it approximates more closely to the biblical view of man. On this account, to have a soul or to be a soul is to be capable of bearing a certain range of qualities. A plant, as opposed to a stone or a piece of metal, has the kind of soul in virtue of which it lives and grows; an animal feels, and a man feels and thinks, in addition. On this view, the "soul" of a man is just that aspect of him in virtue of which he can properly be said to live, grow, feel, and think. There is no question here of his being two things, or one thing using another; he is one thing, to think about which from one point of view is to think about his soul, to think about which from another point of view is to think about his body. In considering a china dish, I can think of it either as china (as a kind of matter with certain physical or chemical properties) or as a dish (as an object with a certain shape and function). But this does not imply that what I think of is really two things, the china and the dish. The difficulty of this point of view, as far as the Christian theist is concerned, is that the claim that the soul survives the body is hard to understand on the basis of it; as the shape and function of the china dish seem to presuppose the continued existence and integrity of the constituent china, so the existence of the soul seems to presuppose that of the body. However, a more central tenet of Christian theism than the survival of the human soul is the resurrection of the human body; this seems arbitrary on the Platonist view, whereas on the Aristotelian one it seems at least at first sight necessary for any form whatever of existence after death.

A few contemporary theologians, not the least influential, treat the question of life after death as irrelevant to Christian theism. What is at issue, they claim, is the relationship with God which men enjoy here and now. But it seems to me that this is a false antithesis; on the traditional view, *both* a relationship with God here and now *and* a life to come are at issue. The importance of the question of life after death for religion has been well expressed by C. D. Broad.[3] It is intrinsic to the belief of most religious believers, he points out, that there should be at least a rough justice in the universe. (The existence of God, as I tried to show above, in one of the senses in which it is understood by traditional Christians, may be held to entail the existence of such cosmic justice.) But nothing could be clearer than that there is no justice, when only the present life, with its flagrant differences in the distribution of health, wealth, and happiness, and the irrelevance of these to any considerations of desert, is taken into account. Hence the question of whether there is, or could possibly be, any evidence for a life after death for at least some human beings, ought to be of interest to believers. The opinion of Broad may be contrasted with that of D. Z. Phillips, who says that the religious idea of immortality has no bearing on the purely secular question of whether there is any life after death.[4] It may be conceded to Phillips that *more* is involved in the Christian doctrine of immortality than life after death in some form or other; but it must be insisted that *at least* this is involved.

There are a number of conceptual difficulties which have been alleged in the idea of life after death. (I shall use the phrase "life after death" here to designate either the survival of the soul or the resurrection of the body, or both.) To expect things to happen to someone after he is dead, it has been said, is to overlook the important fact that he will then no longer exist.[5] In any case, if I say "I will survive bodily death", exactly what do I mean by "I" in this context?[6] Terms like "I", "you", "John", and so on, which refer to persons, refer to entities which can be seen, heard, and touched, just as physical objects can. The very use in our language of terms referring to and describing persons depends on their being identified and re-identified by these means. Now if I say that "we" will continue to exist after our deaths, evidently I do not mean that our bodies will continue to go on functioning as they have previously done, or that they will not disintegrate; because that they will not function as they have previously done, and that they will disintegrate, is precisely what it will be for us to be dead. But if this is the case, what could possibly be meant by the "we" who it is alleged will survive? Persons constitute a sub-class of the class of physical object—if by "physical object" we mean what can be seen, heard, and felt—just as finches are a sub-class of the class of birds. Thus to say that persons, or the particular person designated by each of the words "I" and "you" and "John", survive bodily death, seems very like saying, of a dead finch, that though the bird is dead, the finch continues to exist. Obviously this is nonsense.

It has been suggested that belief in the immortality of the soul should be regarded as an expression of the conviction that there is a special importance in human life, and therefore a special significance in human death, such as cannot be attributed to a mere fact of professional interest to a physiologist or anatomist.[7] But even if this is so, it remains that the proposition that persons, or some persons, enjoy life after death, must be examined on its own merits as a proposition; after all, a moment's reflection will show that its truth or falsity is distinct from our envisagement of human beings as specially privileged among physical objects, and as such that we condemn the kind of treatment of them (say, as mere tools or mere experimental animals) which neglects this special significance. Whatever the belief of life after death may *express*, in terms of men's agony and hope about the death of those they love, it does make a factual claim; and the reassurance and comfort which it gives to the bereaved depends on the fact that it does so. The mere assurance that all will somehow be well is not to the point; the comfort given to the bereaved by the doctrine of life after death depends on its implication that they will be re-united with those whom they have loved and lost, and this presupposes the expectation of life after death for those already dead and (presumably) for the bereaved.[8]

Many Christian believers cheerfully admit that all these difficulties in the doctrine of the soul's survival of bodily death are insoluble, holding rightly that the traditional Church, following the New Testament itself, places far more emphasis on hope of the resurrection of the body—that is, the reconstitution of the human person as a whole. And even A. J. Ayer in *Language, Truth and Logic*, while arguing that the proposition that the soul survived bodily death was meaningless, admitted that the doctrine of the resurrection of the body was at least meaningful, however grossly improbable.[9] But here too there are conceptual difficulties. By what token could it definitively be claimed, of a person in all respects like John Smith who was reconstituted some thousands of years after the death of John Smith, that this actually *was* John Smith, and not merely an imitation of him?[10] Every particle of matter in our bodies is supposed to change every few years, in any case; so, when I say that I am the same person as someone who did certain things at a certain school twenty years ago, I do not imply that any fragment of my present body was actually in that place at that time. But I do imply that there is a spatio-temporal continuity between the man writing this chapter here and now and the boy doing certain things then and there. But, in the case of a person allegedly reconstituted long after his death, there could be no such spatio-temporal continuity between the individual at the earlier and at the later time.

Neither the objections to the doctrine of the soul's survival of death, nor those to that of the resurrection of the body, seem to me to be insuperable. Even if it is true, moreover, that the doctrine of the resurrection of the body is more central to Christian theism[11] than that of the survival of the soul, it does not follow that the Christian theist need accept the logical arguments against the survival of the soul as valid, whether he actually believes in the doctrine or not, unless they seem to be so on their own merits. In the case of physical objects, we expect a spatio-temporal continuity between object A at time T1 and object B at time T2 if we admit that they are one and the same. In the case of persons, we also expect, at least in normal cases, a continuity of memory in addition; each of us can test this directly in himself by introspection (one has the characteristic feeling of being the man who caused an academic scandal some years ago), and infer it in others from what they say. Presumably the disembodied soul of someone deceased would have to remember having been that person, or, perhaps better, having been an aspect of that person, in order for it to be properly said that it *was* that person's disembodied soul. (For a Platonist, to whom the soul is itself the person, the soul would remember having been a person using a body; for an Aristotelian, a soul could remember at most having been an aspect of a person.) This brings us to the question of exactly what it is that could be meaningfully claimed to survive bodily death, whether we are to call it a person or an aspect of a person. Evidently, so far as to be a person is to be a body, persons cannot properly be said to survive death and the dissolution of the body. But it may be claimed that there is an aspect of each person which is in some sense distinct from his body; and consequently that we can make significant statements about a person which cannot be translated without remainder into statements about his body. Let us define a "body" as that aspect of a person by virtue of which he is or could conceivably be observable to others. It may be admitted then that the criteria of bodily identity are the same as those for any physical object. In that case the question is whether there are any statements about persons which cannot be translated without remainder into statements about what is publicly observable. Now it seems to me that there plainly are such statements. Suppose I feel an ache in a certain part of my jaw. This ache as such could never be publicly observable. It may always be the case *in fact* that when I feel such an ache there is a piece of tissue that an incision or an X-ray photograph will reveal to be defective; but there is no logical necessity that this should be the case. However many times I have had pain and the tissue has been observed by a doctor to be defective in a particular way, it would never be self-contradictory for me to claim that I have the pain, while admitting that the usual physical correlate of the pain is not present in this instance. It is similarly true of all statements about a person's experience that they are not equivalent in meaning to any statement about his publicly-observable body, since, however many times a type of experience X were found conjoined with a physical event in the body Y, it would never be a contradiction to claim that in a particular case X had occurred and not Y. It may in fact be the case, and research may tend to confirm this hypothesis more and more, that every experience has a physical correlate; but it could never be the case that experiences were found to be identical with their physical correlates—except perhaps on a special understanding of the meaning of "identical" invented *ad hoc* to obliterate the difficulty.[12] It thus seems to be logically possible that there could be a series of experiences linked by memory but without physical correlates; and the subject of such experiences would be a disembodied soul.

That a "private language" is impossible,[13] that language depends essentially on a shared public world, and on publicly observable criteria for the ascription of qualities to persons, has seemed to some to rule out the possibility of the existence of such irreducibly private events as I have described. But that a private language is impossible does not entail that there cannot be an aspect of public language which refers to and describes private facts, always assuming that these have characteristic (though not necessarily invariable) publicly observable correlates. If our private states, for instance of pain, did not have characteristic public occasions and expressions, we could certainly never have learned to talk about pain as we do; our talk about pain depends on the fact that we react physically to certain situations affecting our bodies in the same kind of way as other people do to similar situations affecting theirs, and that in these situations we feel pain. Thus, since something irreducibly private has characteristic physical occasions and manifestations, people can learn from one another how to use a public language to talk about it. A disembodied soul might enjoy a series of private experiences linked by memory to those of a "person" in the full sense of the term—a conscious rational being who was part of the physical world—without itself being part of it.

Alleged cases of multiple personality provide interesting examples of what may conceivably happen when the usual criteria of personal identity, bodily continuity and continuity of memory and overall consistency of character, get out of alignment with one another. In the celebrated case described in the book *The*

Three Faces of Eve,[14] there were three distinct characters, each with its own series of memories, sharing one body at different times. (The advertisement on the cover of the book describes the case as one of "three women in one body", but this seems to me to presuppose an unduly Platonist point of view. It would surely be better described as three souls in one body.) Eve White was a worried, nervous, conscientious person who had occasional periods of blackout; Eve Black was feckless, irresponsible, and fond of a good time; she took over the body of Eve White during the latter's periods of blackout and seemed to know, as though she were intimately acquainted with her, what Eve White thought and felt, though Eve White showed no such knowledge of her. Jane had an intimate knowledge of the character of both Eve White and Eve Black, and was witness of their activities as though as a detached observer; she was mature and capable in character, quite unlike either Eve White or Eve Black. Finally, after an acute emotional crisis, a character emerged who shared qualities of all three, and moreover remembered having been all three. Now even if the book which I have summarized were a work of fiction, which it is not, it would be worth careful consideration as an example of how the usual criteria of personal identity might conceivably become divorced from one another; and hence of how the question, "Were there three persons involved, or only one?", might not admit of a clear answer.

Incidentally, the final issue of this curious case suggests how sense might be made of the doctrine of reincarnation. The great logical stumbling-block to this doctrine, as far as I can see, is that it is difficult to understand the proposition that B, or the soul of B, living at a later time, is really the same as A, or the soul of A, living at an earlier time, unless B remembers having been A; and this is not, except perhaps very rarely, claimed of particular instances of reincarnation by upholders of the doctrine. But sense might be given to the notion if it were postulated that at some still later time there should be a person C, who remembered having been both A and B, even though B could not remember having been A. It might be objected that it would be systematically impossible to separate such claims from the mere vivid exercise of the historical imagination, or from delusion; but one can imagine successive historical confirmations, for example in the case of one who claimed to be the reincarnation of a personage about whom there were substantial historical records (to which, of course, access by the person himself would have to be ruled out), which could accumulate in such a way as to make these alternative explanations more and more implausible. But the question of the logical possibility of reincarnation, though full of points of philosophical interest, is relevant to Christian theism only as throwing light on the concept of the soul in general; so it cannot be dealt with at length here.

The criteria of identity for a disembodied or reincarnated soul, as having been the soul of a particular person who existed in the past, would apply *a fortiori* to a reconstituted person or resurrected body. The resurrected John Smith would presumably both remember having been John Smith, and have a character like John Smith, and have physical characteristics resembling those of John Smith. (How close these correspondences in character and physical constitution would have to be is impossible to settle *a priori*; but clearly, the more unlike he was admitted to be to John Smith in any of these ways, the less sense there would be in saying he really was John Smith.) To the objection that the allegedly resurrected John Smith might only be a copy of the original John Smith, and not the man himself,[15] it could be answered that one crucial differentiating criterion would be whether he remembered having been John Smith. There are some difficulties about this criterion. It might be objected, for instance, that to say that a man remembers having been John Smith is to assume that he was John Smith; since one of the conditions of the truth of the proposition "I remember being run over five years ago", as opposed to that of "I seem to remember being run over five years ago", or "I have as it were a memory of being run over five years ago", is that I actually *was* run over five years ago. On this reckoning, since X's remembering that he was John Smith *implies* that he really was John Smith, it cannot be taken as *evidence* of the claim that he was. But this objection can be met, I think, if the statement about the relation of X's memory to John Smith is made with more care. Within the bounds of the present life, one of the principal criteria determining whether Y's apparent memory that he was Jack Jones really represents the truth, is a genuine memory or not, is whether there is a spatio-temporal continuity between Y's body and that of Jack Jones. This would not apply in the case of a resurrected body or reconstituted person, since *ex hypothesi* there would be no spatio-temporal continuity. (It might be, of course, that the actual particles of matter which constituted the body of Jack Jones at some point in his life later constituted the body of Y at some point in his; but this does not seem to be a promising candidate as a criterion for personal identity, since according to it I may be, for all I know, identical with Dr. Johnson.) However, another important criterion is whether Y, as well as having an apparent memory of having been Jack Jones, claims to remember a series of trivial incidents in Jack Jones's life, such as it would be reasonable for only Jack Jones to know, which Y could not have obtained information about in any ordinary way, but which turn out actually to have taken place. This kind of criterion of identity could apply between a person and his allegedly reconstituted self, and does not presuppose what it is meant to establish.

The upshot of my argument so far is that belief in life after death for all or some men, either as disembodied souls or as resurrected bodies or as both in succession, is quite logically coherent. It might be asked further what grounds there could possibly be for the belief. Apart from divine revelation, the most obvious claimant to provide such grounds is psychical research. As with the problem of the occurrence of miracles, it seems to me that the common attempt to dismiss all the evidence on *a priori* grounds is ill-judged. The evidence should be considered piecemeal. Much of it seems to suggest that the souls of at least some of the dead continue to exist, since they succeed under some conditions in communicating with the living. The question which ought to be asked is whether fraud, credulity, and coincidence can account for all the alleged evidence; and whether there is some other hypothesis or hypotheses than the activity of disembodied souls that can account for any phenomena that cannot plausibly be dismissed in this way.[16] There is a great deal of wishful thinking on this subject, working against as well as for acceptance of the theory of the soul's survival of bodily death. There is no doubt that many people would be far happier if they could find conclusive evidence for an afterlife; but at the same time its possibility is grossly inconsistent with the scientific world-view as generally understood, and therefore offensive to the sensibility of those whose emotions are bound up with this, quite apart from the validity or otherwise of the alleged evidence for it. It is notoriously difficult to approach this subject with a really open mind; but one of those with the best claim to have done so, the philosopher, C. D. Broad, has confessed that, on the basis of the evidence he has studied, his psychical aspect will be rather more annoyed than surprised to find itself surviving his bodily death.[17]

If disembodied souls ever communicate with us, it seems that they do so by manipulating physical things in our environment as signs; and it might be objected that it is inconceivable that an immaterial agent could have such an effect on material objects. But those who say that such activity is *inconceivable*, as opposed to merely *impossible*, should consider such examples as the following.[18] Suppose that a man arrives at his office one morning, when the door has been locked all night and his friends do not have keys to it, to find in his typewriter a message purporting to be from a deceased acquaintance, concluding with a promise to communicate with him in the same manner the next night. Naturally suspecting some kind of deception, the man sprinkles flour on the floor of his office, and fastens threads across the door, before he goes home in the evening; but the promised message duly appears when he returns the next morning, though the threads have apparently not been snapped and the flour has not been disturbed. The message concludes with a promise to communicate yet again the next night. By this time the affair has attracted a certain amount of attention among people of the district who are interested in occult phenomena; and a team of them accordingly undertake to observe a vigil at the man's office the next night. While one of them is watching during the small hours, a piece of paper is seen to move into the typewriter, the roller to turn until the paper is appropriately placed, and the keys to be depressed one by one. While this is going on, the watcher gropes just above the keys of the typewriter; but his fingers encounter no resistance. Now I do not suppose that a course of events quite like this has ever actually occurred; but it does appear to me to be perfectly conceivable. And it is difficult to see how else it could be plausibly accounted for, except in terms of activity of a disembodied spirit. To say that must be a very rarefied material being is to say nothing, unless there were suggested some physical tests, apart from the results of its activity in getting the message written, which would detect its presence.

This example has a resemblance to Professor Wisdom's well-known parable of the gardener and, like it, might seem to issue in the conclusion that the choice between saying "A disembodied soul did this", and "It just came out like this", was merely a choice between one manner of speaking and another. In Wisdom's parable, two men find a clearing in a forest; one of them says that the arrangement of the flowers and shrubs there suggests that a gardener must come to work there, while the other denies this. In order to settle the dispute they decide to set trip-wires and other devices such that any intruder is bound to betray his presence; but when these produce no result, the believer in the gardener refuses to give up his hypothesis, only qualifying it by conceding that the gardener is invisible and intangible. But once such qualifications have been made, one begins to wonder whether anything more is at issue between the disputants than a mere subjective way of looking at the phenomena in question which makes no claims whatsoever about any matter of fact.[19] But there is a crucial difference between my example and Wisdom's parable. Whereas, in the parable, the situation was such that at first sight there was room for difference of opinion, the events in the example were such that, until a great deal of checking and testing had been gone through, no one in his senses would wish to deny that they were due to the activity of a rational agent.

Flew says that with the doctrine of life after death, as with so many of the tenets of religion, the sceptic's first difficulty is with the *meaning*, rather than with the truth or falsity, of what is claimed.[20] I have argued here that the doctrine is meaningful in both its usual forms, and hence that there is a real question, as with the doctrines of the existence of God and the occurrence of miracles, of whether it is true or false. I have repeatedly claimed, in the earlier chapters of this book, that the Christian faith has eschatological truth-conditions; here I have tried to show that eschatological statements, so far as they bear on any form of human afterlife, do at least make sense.

7 CONCLUSION

The arguments which I have put forward in this book are based on the fundamental premiss that to be a theist is to construe the world as a whole on the model of the activities of a rational agent. To be a Christian theist, at least in the traditional sense, is to believe that this agent has done, is doing, and will do certain particular things; which in turn entails that these particular things have happened, are happening, and will happen. Thus the Christian theist's claims may come into conflict with those of certain scientists, especially, as it happens, historians. The particular claims as to matters of fact which characterize traditional Christian theism, like the truth-conditions of a scientific hypothesis, differentiate it from a view of the world which merely expresses a moral or aesthetic attitude, but which makes no claim to objective truth.

I have tried to show that arguments to the effect that Christian belief, as so conceived, is incoherent, are ill-founded. The question of its truth or falsity is a different matter; though I have not purported to resolve it, I have suggested the way in which historical evidence might converge in future in such a way as to put the matter beyond all reasonable doubt.

Kai Nielsen's paper *Language and the Concept of God*[1] is an admirably clear and concise example of a very common kind of attack on theistic belief by contemporary philosophers. A summary of my overall defence of the logical coherence of such belief may thus conveniently take the form of a rebuttal of objections which he raises. His argument is briefly as follows. Traditional theism, with its crude doctrine of God as a kind of cosmic superman[2] is too obviously false, in the same kind of way as beliefs in ghosts and witches are,[3] to be believed by people who understand the general bearing of the science and philosophy of the twentieth century. A qualified and attenuated form of theism is therefore advanced by some contemporary philosophers and theologians, of whom J. A. T. Robinson and D. Z. Phillips are notable examples. This kind of theism, however, may be seen on investigation to make no coherent sense.[4] Now I agree with Nielsen that no advantage is gained by one who purports to remain a Christian theist while rejecting all the factual presuppositions of Christian theism; such a move at worst makes nonsense of Christian theism, at best reduces it to a picture of the world and of human life possibly desirable to some on aesthetic grounds, but with no conceivable claim to objective truth. Such a way of talking, it seems to me, is rather like insisting that phlogiston exists, while accepting all the experimental evidence which ultimately induced chemists to abandon the concept. But I shall try to defend against Nielsen's objections a kind of Christian theism which, while quite capable of articulation in terms which make sense to a sophisticated modern man, does not abandon the factual claims which have traditionally characterized it. I shall label this kind of belief "sophisticated traditional theism", and such systems of belief as those of Phillips and Robinson, which do tend to abandon these factual claims, as "reductionist theism". To be a traditional theist, whether sophisticated or unsophisticated, is to envisage the events of which nature and history consist as being the result of the actions of an intelligent and benevolent agent, and hence to believe that things and events have turned out, are turning out, and will turn out, in a certain very general way. Such theists as Phillips and Robinson, while trying to defend theism, make it independent of such factual claims,[5] and thus make it more rather than less vulnerable to objections like those alleged by Nielsen.

According to the sophisticated traditional theist, as opposed to the reductionist, that which makes all the things and brings about all the events of which nature and history consist, *has* brought about particular states of affairs in the past (pre-eminently, the life, death, and resurrection of Jesus Christ for Christians, and the delivery of the children of Israel from Egypt for Jews), and *will* bring about certain states of affairs in the future (such that the mourners will be comforted, the merciful obtain mercy, and the meek inherit the earth). Nielsen sees orthodox Jews and Christians praying to "God" and confessing their sins to him, wonders to whom or to what they are praying and confessing, and finally admits himself at a loss.[6] Here is the answer. They are praying to that which brings about the events of nature and history, and which has shown by particular signs in the past (the life of Jesus and the

Exodus) its gracious purposes for man in the future. According to Nielsen,

> Providence, the benevolent guidance of God, no longer means for sophisticated believers that some supernatural reality, some creative source of all reality other than itself, is directing the scene so that we can discover in the way things go the loving "hand of God". Natural disasters or moral calamities are no longer thought to call Divine Providence into question.[7]

Now there is a vital difference, oddly neglected by Nielsen, between a sophisticated traditional theist like Aquinas, Barth, Rahner, or Lonergan; and a reductionist theist like Bultmann, Phillips, or Robinson. The sophisticated traditional theist *does* believe in just the kind of providence that Nielsen describes, though he is likely to admit that the operation of this providence is not immediately to be inferred from the facts of present human experience; to see it as operating here and now is to be committed to a faith about how things will ultimately turn out. Natural and moral disasters may indeed, as Basil Mitchell has said, count somewhat against such a belief,[8] but the sophisticated traditional theist would plead that they do not count decisively against it. And he thinks that he sees signs of the operation of this providence both in the history of Jesus Christ and in the experience he has of God's graciousness in his own life.

Thus there is no difficulty whatever for the sophisticated traditional theist in saying "what the difference is between what one believes being true and what one believes not being true", in compliance with Bernard Williams' requirement.[9] He believes that certain particular events have happened in the past, and that a certain state of affairs is to be brought about in the future. His present experience of God, through his private devotion and in the fellowship of the Church, gives him confidence that God will indeed act according to his promises. "After death we shall have no consciousness at all," Nielsen tells us;[10] but this is precisely one of the crucial points at issue between the atheistic humanist and the traditional theist. It has indeed been argued by some that the very conception of life after death for any man, whether as a disembodied soul or as a resurrected body, is incoherent; I have already attacked some of these arguments.

Nielsen is quite right to say that "to understand the word 'God', as it is used in Jewish and Christian contexts, is to understand what it would be like for 'God created man in his image and likeness' or 'In God alone is man sustained' to be true";[11] but he objects that neither believers nor unbelievers can understand what is meant by these expressions "once they give up an anthropomorphic conception of divinity". I am not at all sure what Nielsen means by an anthropomorphic conception of divinity (not that there is any general difficulty with the notion; a view of God like that of Cleanthes in Hume's *Dialogues* is an obvious example); but in as far as it implies that God is a material being or a creature I certainly would not wish to defend it, and therefore will confine myself to such explanations as might be offered by the sophisticated traditional theist. By "God" is meant that of whose actions the universe consists. Thus, if God did not exist and act there would be no universe and no man; this is what it is for man to depend for his existence totally on, to be sustained by, God. The whole universe is the sphere of God's intelligent activity; a very small part of it is the sphere of intelligent activity of each particular man; thus man, whose activity in a small sphere is comparable to God's activity in an indefinitely larger one, is to that extent "in the image and likeness" of God.[12] That God acts according to the particular general patterns discovered in our environment by scientific inquiry is what it is for him to have "created" just *this* universe.[13] Naturally, his mode of existence is independent as compared with the things that constitute the universe, which depend wholly on this existence and activity; this is implied, among other things, by the statement that God's existence is "necessary" as opposed to "contingent".[14] The God of traditional Christianity is, *pace* Tillich and Robinson, inevitably "supranatural",[15] if we mean by the sphere of the "natural" the results of the normal activity of the divine agent, so far as we can be aware of them, as opposed to his exceptional actions, and to the divine agent himself.

Robinson quite correctly represents traditional theism when he says that love is at the heart of things, in the very grain of the universe;[16] but he does not sufficiently draw out the consequences of his assertion, which are that the ultimate fate of human beings will not be what it would appear to be at first sight—on the contrary, that the mourners will be comforted and the merciful obtain mercy. Now if this were to take place, it could only take place in some kind of afterlife, since no synthetic proposition is more certain than that it does not take place in this one. But Robinson, so far as I can see, does not anywhere, at least in his better-known books, commit himself to the unequivocal assertion that there is an afterlife. As it stands, as Nielsen justly comments,[17] Robinson's statement that love is at the heart of things is so vague that it could be understood in a sense that would be admitted by many atheistic humanists; that human life is such that love in human beings is a beneficial and commendable disposition. Robinson would protest that he means more than this, but does not clearly show *what* more he means. But if for love to be at the heart of things is for the unhappy to be in the future made happy, and the oppressed made free, and those who have striven for virtue rewarded—then the assertion that love is in the very grain of the universe is both such that we can clearly understand what it is for it to be true or false, and goes far beyond what an atheistic humanist could admit without ceasing to be such. Of course this belief in a future salvation comes to a great deal more than the belief, which as Nielsen says humanists may very well hold, that in the process of history the powers of reaction will in the long run be prevailed over by more benevolent and forward-looking policies;[18] though one does not need to be very cynical to comment that, human nature being what it is, there is no good reason to assent to this belief, except on the basis of a prior belief in the sanctifying power of God.

It may be objected that, in my concern to show that Phillips and Robinson have misrepresented traditional theism, I have been too ready to accept uncritically Nielsen's strictures on their position considered on its own merits. In fact, I think that something quite coherent can be made out of their view provided that its exponents resolutely abstain from taking in the washing of the more traditional kind of theism. It might be urged on their behalf that, even if what the traditional Christian alleges has been and will be the case has not been and will not be the case, many persons achieve intrinsically valuable states by praying and engaging in religious rituals, which states are called "knowing God" or "having experience of God". If Nielsen objects that these experiences are illusory one might reply, in the manner of Phillips,[19] that such an objection is only valid on the basis of a clear conception of the criteria of truth and falsity within the realm of discourse concerned.

That some people have these experiences, and that they are intensely valuable to them, seems scarcely possible to deny; and the onus would be on Nielsen to show that talk about God (always provided that the traditional factual presuppositions which have gone with this talk are clearly excluded) is the wrong way of responding to, conveying, and describing such experience. My own objections to reductionist theism are mainly that its purveyors, from Hegel and Schleiermacher to Robinson and Phillips,[20] are not too clear-minded, or at least too frank, about the very radical difference between their own "God" and the God of traditional theism. For instance, on Phillips's view, in which religious practice seems to be quite autonomous and self-justifying, and such that no experience now or in future could conceivably invalidate it (as it can on the traditional view), it would surely be better to say that God is the creation of man than that man is the creation of God. This is because religion is an activity of man, and "God", according to this conception of him, seems to be nothing more than an intentional object of this activity, no more existing outside the human activities of prayer and worship than races exist outside the running of them. And "salvation", which seems to consist of nothing over and above religious experience here and now, is on this account a comparatively trivial option. But much of the charm of reductionist theism is due to the fact that these consequences are not brought out, and that as a result it appears to be much closer to traditional theism than in fact it is.

I anticipate one objection to traditional theism, as I have just outlined it, which might be made by Nielsen: "But even if Jesus acted just as the Gospels say that he did, and even if the ultimate fate of mankind turns out to be in accordance with his promises—this still does not imply that a transcendent God exists." One may compare the following argument: "Whatever movements are made by Jones's body, their occurrence does not necessarily imply the direction of that body by a rational intelligence"; or, "Whatever experience you have as though of a table, it could conceivably be the case that you were deluded and that there was no real table present to your senses." I set my hypothetical opponent a dilemma: *either* he should show that human minds do not transcend (the appropriateness of this term is significant) human physical states and behaviour; *or* he should admit that the being of God as I have described him is not necessarily wholly reducible to those results of his activity which are, according to the theist, the things and events which constitute the universe as we know it. Admittedly, if it did not happen and will not turn out as the traditional theist claims, it is arbitrary of him to insist on talking about nature and history in terms of the activity of "God" (just as it is arbitrary to assert of a physical object that it is the body of a conscious agent when it is admitted that there was, is, and will be nothing in its external behaviour to indicate this); but if events have turned out and will turn out as the theist expects, then it is equally arbitrary to refuse to talk in terms of God's activity.

I have tried to show that in the case of traditional Christian theism it is quite clear what it is for it to be true, what it is for it is to be false. Admittedly it is rather more problematic how far this is possible with regard to the reduced types of theism which are typified by the thought of Robinson and Phillips. But even if Nielsen's arguments tend to show that this kind of theism is incoherent, they certainly do not show the incoherence of traditional theism.

APPENDIX

WHITEHEAD ON GOD AND THE WORLD

Whitehead's philosophical doctrines are derived from prolonged reflection on scientific method, the history of thought, and those aspects of experience of which the scientific world-view in its present state appears to take insufficient account. Also there are signs that his influence in the English-speaking world is growing, after a period of hostility to his thought or comparative neglect of it. It therefore seems worthwhile to conclude this book with a summary of his account of God's relationship with the world. Whitehead's opinions on this subject seem to have changed somewhat during the course of his development; what follows will be based mainly on *Religion in the Making*, with some reference, where elucidation seems necessary, to *Process and Reality*, *Science and the Modern World*, and *Adventures of Ideas*.[1]

Religious dogmas try to formulate in precise terms truths disclosed in the religious experience of mankind, just as science strives to formulate truths disclosed in sense-perception. Now there is by no means agreement within the religious experience of mankind for the existence of a transcendent creator God; but there is a very large consensus in favour of a rightness in things, to some extent conformed to in fact, to some extent denied and frustrated. One has an intuition of conforming or failing to conform to this rightness, and of evil as lack of such conformity.[2]

The term "God" itself may be used with any one of three meanings: (1) the immanent order to which the world more or less conforms; (2) the totality of which the world that we know is an aspect, and of which description of the world that we know is a partial description; or (3) "a definite personal individual entity, whose existence is the one ultimate metaphysical fact, absolute and underivative, and who decreed and ordered the derivative existence which we call the actual world". According to the first conception of God, the extreme doctrine of immanence, to say anything about God is to say something about the world; while according to the second, which is pantheism, to say anything about the world is to say something about God. The difficulty about the third, according to which God is the absolutely transcendent creator, is that it makes God quite unamenable to any form of reasoning based on our acquaintance with and reasoning about the world. Any argument which purports to prove the existence of God or something about his nature, from consideration of the character of the world, cannot penetrate beyond this world. Reason can only reveal all the factors disclosed in the world as we experience it. In other words, it may discover an immanent God, but not a God wholly transcendent.[3]

Jesus inherited from his background the conception of an absolutely transcendent God; on the other hand, he associated with it the idea of a kingdom of heaven within men and the metaphor of fatherhood in the relationship between God and men. The Johannine Gospel and First Epistle, with their conceptions of God as love and as *logos* or rational principle, take further this move towards a doctrine of God as immanent in the universe, and as gently persuading creatures rather than exercising despotic power over them. The Alexandrian school of theologians in the early Church, with their Platonist way of thinking, tended to follow the Johannine lead; unfortunately the Church at large reverted to the idea of God as a transcendent despot, and the gospel of love was consequently changed by and large into one of fear. Much of the tragedy and horror in the history of both Christianity and Islam must be attributed to the dominance of this idea. It is now very widely held that men ought to find God through love rather than fear, but another widespread contemporary dogma, that religious doctrine ought to be simple, is not so justifiable. There is no good metaphysical reason for insisting that the truth about things must be simple. If we are going consistently to follow our rational faculties in determining the truth about the world, we will not impose such *a priori* restrictions on them. Also, simplifications of religious doctrine are all shipwrecked on the problem of evil. On the other hand, we have no good reason to deny that religious experience has something to contribute to our knowledge of the universe; and metaphysics must take account of this contribution. In fact science, metaphysics, and rational religion, must all take account of one another.[4]

Reflection on the world as a whole, which takes scientific, aesthetic, and religious experience into account, reveals it to have the following very general types of formative elements: (1) Creativity or the whole gamut of actual creatures developing themselves through time, by which the world has the characteristic of "temporal passage to novelty"; (2) "ideal entities, or forms"—themselves potential rather than actual existents, yet exemplified in what actually exists (these, which Whitehead calls "eternal objects",[5] are more or less the universals of traditional philosophy); (3) "What men call God", which is "an actual but non-temporal entity whereby the indetermination of mere creativity is transmuted into a determinate freedom". God not only affects everything, but is affected by everything; it is fundamental to Whitehead's view of the universe (as opposed to traditional theism as I have described it) that each thing in it is related to everything else, and needs the context of the universe as a whole in order to exist; and that nothing, even God, can exist all by itself. Apart from the operation of God, however, the other constituent elements of the universe could not be brought into such a relationship as is required for the existence of any definite temporal entity. If it were not for the harmonious order which God provides, the remaining formative elements would fail in their function. We may thus infer his existence and activity from the nature of the world as it confronts us; "the ordering entity is a necessary element in the metaphysical situation presented by the actual world". The conviction that some order is to be found in the universe is the motive force of all scientific inquiry (though indeed a great deal of modern philosophy consists of ingenious arguments to evade this actually inescapable conclusion); and God is that which accounts for this order. It is a mistake to think of God as infinite. If he were, he would be as evil as good, and furthermore would lack the determinateness requisite to influence the course of events as he does. The contemplation of ourselves in relation to God as the source of all order is what gives rise to the feelings of companionship and refreshment aimed at by the religions.[6]

According to Whitehead, "value is inherent in actuality itself", and there is "an ultimate enjoyment of being actual". This view may seem implausible, and it is based on the queer premiss that feeling characterizes everything that exists, not only animals and men. But Whitehead would insist that the queerness of this assumption depends on our irrational tendency to prefer, in our reflections about the ultimate truth of things, the abstractions of the scientist to the deliverances of the poet,[7] and to take seriously our visual at the expense of our visceral sensations. Thus he complains that so-called "empiricism", on the Humean model, distorts and misrepresents what are in fact the most obvious and elementary features of our experience. No one would disagree that feeling is a central feature of the mental life which is characteristic of those most elaborately organized physical objects, human beings; Whitehead asks us, perhaps not wholly implausibly, to accept that lower degrees of physical organization are characterized by feeling of lower intensity.[8] Evil takes the form of physical or mental suffering, or the loss of higher in favour of lower experience. But its occurrence always goes inseparably conjoined with a tendency to self-elimination. "The fact of the instability of evil is the moral order in the world." What is good without qualification is creative; evil is "a descent towards nothingness", occasioned characteristically by the fact that creatures obstruct one another in their self-realization. The instability of evil may lead either to progress, as a result of which higher and more intense degrees of feeling are realized, or to a stage in which the type of thing affected by evil "ceases to exist, or . . . sinks back into a stage in which it ranks below the possibility of that form of evil". (Organization at a particular level of complexity, one might infer, is at first impaired, and at length rendered wholly impossible, so that lower levels of organization are all that are realized. Thus the bad man may sink to the level of an animal, the dead animal to a mere mass of chemical compounds.) God's influence is not coercive—coercion being one of the notes of evil; he influences each thing by the lure of its own possible full development and the ideal of a complete harmony of things. The essential religious insight is that the order of the world, the beauty of the world, and the mastery of evil, are all connected. This is because God is the source of order, as revealed in scientific discovery but also by artistic vision; moral order is one aspect of the general order on the basis of which and towards which God directs the world. (Whitehead says that moral order is one variety of aesthetic order; I suppose he means that the aspects of a bad man jar against one another, and he jars against other members of his society, rather as the aspects of a bad work of art frustrate rather than enhance one another).[9]

In general, Whitehead's God acts upon the world as an artist, as a promoter of an aesthetic order. The order and the "self-contrast with ideals" which we find in the world show the immanence of God in it; on the other hand, its incompleteness and its evil show that it has additional formative elements for which God's activity is not responsible. God not only acts upon the world, but receives a reaction from it; the effects of this reaction upon him make up his "consequent" as opposed to "primordial" nature. God's primordial purpose is to achieve intensity of feeling in the world; this makes him care for each particular entity that is brought into being in the temporal process. The thoroughgoing reciprocity of action between God and the world of creatures in Whitehead's thought, the fact that each is an "instrument of novelty" for the other, and its consequence that God as well as the world is subject to temporal development, is the most radical difference between it and traditional theism.[10]

The differences between Whitehead's view of God and the traditional one seem mainly due to two fundamental problems in theism, those of transcendence and evil. According to Whitehead, if it is claimed that our reasonings based on our knowledge of the world give us any idea of who or what God is or whether he exists, it must be admitted that he is immanent in the world; to say that he is transcendent of the world is implicitly to deny the relevance of such reasoning. And from God's immanence it follows that the rest of the world may act upon God, just as God may act upon the rest of the world. But it seems to me that there is no reason to accept the basic dilemma. To envisage the world as consisting of the actions of God as agent is to be capable of discussing rationally the nature of God *as* the agent of such actions, on the basis of what we know of the actions; this corresponds to Aquinas' statement that philosophy, or reasoning based on our experience of the world, can show us what is true of God as cause of the world.[11] This account has the merit of showing precisely what is meant by God's "transcendence", and hence how one can state that God transcends the world without implying that he is wholly unintelligible. So far as the world as a whole is envisaged as the actions of God as agent, and so far as one may properly talk about the nature of an agent on the basis of his actions, we may properly talk about God on the basis of what we know about the world, without God being either a part of the world or one formative element in it among others.

In dealing with the problem of evil, Whitehead frankly limits God's power in order to preserve his goodness. As J. B. Cobb says, Whitehead's doctrine stems from the fact that he held that the object of proper religious veneration is "characterized more decisively by goodness than by metaphysical ultimacy".[12] Certainly, on the traditional view, since the existence of the universe is due to the activity of God alone, the occurrence of evil is more directly attributable to God's activity than it is on Whitehead's view; consequently, it may be inferred that the goodness of God according to Whitehead is more closely analogous to human moral goodness than it can be according to the traditional conception. It is part of what we mean by the goodness of a human moral agent, as I have said, that a good human moral agent does not permit evils to occur in matters under his control, except as a necessary means to greater good than would otherwise be possible. Whitehead's God is not so absolutely in control of everything as is the transcendent creator of the Christian tradition, and the evils that exist may thus be attributed to principles which exist in some sense independently of him.[13]

Whitehead's distinction between God's primordial and consequent natures has a bearing on the idea of grace and of God's action upon creatures in general. On the traditional view, as worked out most fully by Aquinas, God acts on each creature according to the sort of creature he has made it to be, and accordingly saves the rational creature by rational persuasion;[14] this deference of God to the nature of the creature, as one might call it, is what does duty in Aquinas' philosophy for Whitehead's doctrine of God's consequent nature. But the distinction as it stands in Whitehead is unnecessary for Aquinas, since he thinks of God as viewing the whole passage of time from an eternal vantage-point, and hence not having to depend on the passage of time and the outcome of temporal contingencies to determine his course of action.[15]

NOTES

INTRODUCTION

1. Cf. the masterly analysis in Karl Barth's *Church Dogmatics* (III, I, pp. 392–414) of the history of the argument to God's existence from the presence of design in the universe. Barth believes that all apologetic arguments which start from the unbeliever's own ground will end up by distorting the belief of the believer; but I think he is going too far in this.
2. As represented, say, in Karl Popper's *The Logic of Scientific Discovery*.
3. Cf. especially the two volumes of *Kerygma and Myth*, by Bultmann and others, and *Existence and Faith*, a collection of Bultmann's shorter writings edited by Schubert M. Ogden.
4. The Eddington Memorial Lecture for 1955.
5. Cf. *Symbols of Transformation*, Vol. 5 of the Collected Works, p. 356.
6. Matthew 5.4, 7.

CHAPTER 1

1. *Church Dogmatics* I, 1, 448 f.
2. Cf. Aquinas, *De Potentia*, III, 7: "God operates in all natural and voluntary activity".
3. *Church Dogmatics* III, I, 365.
4. I. Kant, *Critique of Pure Reason*, p. 346 (*Everyman* edition). It is as well to mention Kant's labels for these arguments, because they have stuck. However, they are in many ways misleading. The "cosmological" argument, for example, might less deceptively have been called the "ontological", since it raises questions of "ontology" in the sense of an inquiry into the ultimate constituents of reality.
5. Many disputes about the meaning of Anselm's famous argument in the *Proslogion* turn on the question of which of these two interpretations should be placed on it.
6. Cf. J. A. T. Robinson, *Honest to God*, p. 13.
7. *Summa Theologica* I, ii, 3.
8. pp. 9 f.
9. Cf. *A Treatise of Human Nature* I, iii, 14.
10. Cf. E. Gilson, *The Philosophy of Saint Thomas Aquinas*, p. 64.
11. op. cit., p. 11.
12. *Summa Theologica* I, xiii, 10.
13. *God and Philosophy*, *passim*.
14. "Dialogue between Richard and Gregory", *Theoria to Theory*, Autumn 1966.
15. A. G. N. Flew, *God and Philosophy*, 3.20.

16. H. Wheeler Robinson, *Inspiration and Revelation in the Old Testament*, p. 1. God is not "physical" since physical objects can be acted upon as well as acting, are operand-transforms as well as operators.
17. Funk and Wagnall, *New Standard Dictionary of the English Language*.
18. op. cit., 3.15–16; cf. R. W. Hepburn, *Christianity and Paradox*, p. 5.
19. *Frontiers of Astronomy*, p. 321.
20. *Religion and the Scientists*, ed. Mervyn Stockwood, p. 56.
21. *Summa Theologica* I, xlvi, 2.
22. Cf. Flew, op. cit., 4.15.
23. J. N. Findlay, "Can God's Existence be Disproved?", *New Essays in Philosophical Theology*, ed. A. G. N. Flew and A. C. MacIntyre, p. 518.
24. *Dialogues Concerning Natural Religion*, 11; cf. Aquinas, *Summa Theologica* I, xiii, 2.
25. This would depend on a more radical conception of freedom than is accepted by many philosophers; cf. pp. 47–56, below.
26. The Molinist school of Catholic theologians referred to this special kind of divine knowledge as *scientia media*.
27. pp. 60–1, below.
28. pp. 75–6, 81–3, below.
29. Cf. A. J. Ayer, *Language, Truth and Logic*, p. 119.
30. The theologies of Schleiermacher and Bultmann, respectively, show the consequences of basing the concept of God too exclusively on religious experience or on human achievement of authentic existence.
31. *The Future of an Illusion*, p. 77. Sometimes he is, from his own point of view, more sanguine; suggesting that religion in humanity, like neurotic traits in the normal adolescent, will inevitably lose its grip as mankind approaches maturity.
32. *The Future of an Illusion*, p. 30; *Civilization and its Discontents*, 23 f.
33. Bultmann and Tillich are perhaps the most distinguished of the modern theologians who present Christian belief as though it had no reference to any future life.
34. *Dialogues*, especially parts I–VIII.
35. *Religion without Revelation*, p. 19.
36. The classical exposition in English of this view, now not very fashionable among philosophers, is A. J. Ayer's *Language, Truth and Logic*.
37. Cf. R. Bambrough, *Religion and Humanism*, p. 61.
38. Not that these ideas have lacked brilliant defenders among contemporary philosophers. For the behaviourist reduction of mental phenomena, cf. G. Ryle, *The Concept of Mind*; for the physicalist, cf. J. J. C. Smart, *Philosophy and Scientific Realism*. But both forms of reduction are open to objections which there is no room to do more than mention here. More will be said on this subject in chapter 6.
39. Ayer, when he wrote *Language, Truth and Logic*, defended the heroic thesis that they were (p. 102).
40. *Science and the Modern World*, p. 179.
41. *Philosophical Analysis*, p. 6.
42. I take this analogy from Donald Hudson's *Ludwig Wittgenstein*, p. 68.

Hudson says it is difficult to set out the difference in kind between such a story and belief in God; but it seems to me that the difficulty remains only so long as one's attention is concentrated upon discourse about God as merely a language-game that *can* be played, and one forgets the particular beliefs in and expectations of matters of fact which have traditionally made the game seem worth playing. A very deft delineation of the stance-towards-life account of religious belief is provided by R. M. Hare, *New Essays in Philosophical Theology*, ed. Flew and MacIntyre, pp. 99–103.

43. Cf. Flew, ibid., pp. 96–9, 106–8.
44. I discuss this at some length, giving examples, in *The New Theology and Modern Theologians*, pp. 133–6.
45. The references are to the numbered paragraphs of *God and Philosophy*.
46. Calvin's theology is the most notable exception to the rule.
47. This question of freedom will be dealt with in detail in chapter 2 below.
48. Chapters 2 and 4 below.
49. The problem is dealt with at length in chapter 3 below.
50. Cf. Velecky, L. C., Flew on Aquinas, *Philosophy* (1968), 212–30.
51. *Summa Theologica* I, ii, I.
52. *The New Creation*, p. 3.
53. "Ultimate concern" is an idea of central importance in the theology of Tillich.
54. "Theology and Falsification"; *New Essays in Philosophical Theology*, ed. Flew and MacIntyre, 96–9, 106–8.
55. *New Essays in Philosophical Theology*, pp. 129 f.
56. *Religion and Understanding*, ed. D. Z. Phillips, p. 1.
57. Col. 3.2 f.; 1 Cor. 15.14–19; Matt. 5.3–10, 25.1–30.
58. Kierkegaard, *Philosophical Fragments*, 45, 51 f., 87.
59. Cf. *Kerygma and Myth*, I, 117.
60. Cf. B. G. Mitchell, "The Justification of Religious Belief" (*Philosophical Quarterly*, 1961, 213–26). Mitchell stigmatizes "a set of false alternatives, between conversion and argument, deciding freely and having reasons, applying rules of logic and being non-rational" (213).

CHAPTER 2

1. Cf. 1 Cor. 15.22; Rom. 8.3; 1 John 2.15.
2. Rom. 7.21 f.
3. Rom. 1.18.
4. 2 Cor. 5.17; Gal. 6.2.
5. Gal. 5.22.
6. Rom. 5—6.
7. Matt. 12.25–9.
8. 2 Cor. 1.22.
9. Eph. 2.6; Col. 1.27.
10. 1 Cor. 15.19.
11. Matt. 5.3–10, 25.31–46; Luke 6.20–6.

12. Cf. especially J. Moltmann, *Theology of Hope*.
13. *Systematic Theology*, I, 55.
14. *Sacramentum Mundi*, II, p. 106 (in the article on *Dogma*).
15. *Theological Investigations*, II, pp. 1–88.
16. *Significando causant*.
17. *Summa Theologica* I, cv, 5.
18. The Roman Catholic theologian Karl Rahner argues that in a sense an unbaptized person in a state of grace belongs to the Church without knowing it (*Theological Investigations*, II, p. 22).
19. *Le Milieu Divin*, 23, 52, etc.
20. Cf. Hobbes, *Leviathan*, II, 21; Hume, *Treatise of Human Nature*, II, iii, I and 2.
21. Cf. Calvin, *Institutes of the Christian Religion*, III, 21–4; 1.18.
22. I Timothy ii.4.
23. "Responsibility and Avoidability", in *Determinism and Freedom in the Age of Modern Science*, ed. Sidney Hook; pp. 157–9.
24. ibid., 158.
25. My colleague Martin Milligan has suggested that it is intrinsic to the notion of complete explanation of any event that all alternatives should be excluded. There seems to me no reason to assume this, except on the hypothesis of determinism. The libertarian may assume that in all cases of genuine human responsibility, both the actual choice and the actions excluded by the choice will be capable of explanation, even when all the preconditions are taken into account.
26. *Enquiry Concerning Human Understanding*, VIII.
27. Cf. W. B. Gallie, *Explanations in History and the Genetic Sciences*, Mind, 1955, p. 177.
28. Cf. the suggestions at the end of J. C. Eccles' *The Neurophysiological Basis of Mind*.
29. Gen. 1.27.
30. Cf. *Poltergeists*, by R. Thurston, S.J.
31. I have tried to summarize the main positions on grace and free will among Christians in *Grace versus Nature*, pp. 258 ff.
32. De pecc. mer. et remiss. II, xviii, 28.
33. Rom. 7.19.
34. Cf. for example, McCord and Zola, *Origins of Crime*.
35. De corr. et grat. xi.
36. *The City of God* XII, 17 (Healey's translation).
37. *Summa Theologica* I, cv, 5.
38. Cf. Rom. 8.28.
39. III *Contra Gentiles*, 160 (T. Gilby's translation).
40. *Summa Theologica* Ia, xlviii, 4; IaIIae, lxxxv, 2.
41. Matt. 7.1.
42. Cf. Barbour, *Issues in Science and Religion*, p. 445.
43. In *Freedom of the Will* (Yale University Press 1957).
44. op. cit., 255–9.
45. Boethius, *De consolatione philosophiae*, v, 6; quoted W. Kneale, *Time and Eternity in Theology*, Proc. Ar. Soc., 1961, 87–108.

46. *Summa Theologica*, I, xix, 8; xiv, 13. Cf. B. Lonergan, "St Thomas on *Gratia Operans*" (especially *Theological Studies* III, 542; 545 f.).
47. Cf. A. N. Prior, *The Modalities of Omniscience* (*Philosophy* 1962, 114–29); also the articles by Nelson Pike and M. McC. Adams in the *Philosophical Review*, 1965 (27–46) and 1967 (492–503).

CHAPTER 3

1. *Church Dogmatics*, III, 3, 295 f. I have discussed at length Barth's account of evil in *Grace versus Nature*, 180–4.
2. 306.
3. 349, 356.
4. 104, 108 ff.
5. III, 2, 143.
6. Cf. my arguments on the explanation of human action in the previous chapter.
7. *Church Dogmatics*, III, 3, 295 ff.
8. Cf. Tillich's very sensible remarks in his *Systematic Theology*, I, 64.
9. Cf. D. M. MacKinnon, *Borderlands of Theology*, 155.
10. S.T. I, xlviii, 2.
11. S.T. I, lxlviii; C.G. III, 12.
12. S.T. I, lxv, 1.
13. S.T. I, xlviii, 2, T. Gilby's translation.
14. *Evil and the God of Love*, pp. 369–72.
15. p. 27.
16. *The City of God*, XI, 18; cf. XII, 4.114. XII, 17.
17. XI, 22.
18. S.T. I, xlviii, 5.
19. S.T. I, xlviii, 6.
20. S.T. I, xlviii, 1.
21. S.T. I, xlviii, 4.
22. S.T. Ia IIae, lxxxv, 2.
23. S.T. IIa IIae, xxviii, 3.
24. "Evil and Omnipotence", *Mind* 1955, pp. 200–12.
25. All italics mine.
26. ibid., 200–2.
27. ibid., 205.
28. ibid., 207 f.
29. ibid., 207 f.
30. My italics; ibid., 208 f.
31. My italics; ibid., 208 f.
32. pp. 47–56, above.
33. John 16.33.
34. "Omnipotence, Evil and Supermen", *Philosophy* (1961), 188–95.
35. *New Essays in Philosophical Theology*, ed. Flew and MacIntyre, p. 96.
36. Cf. pp. 20–1, above.
37. Cf. Aquinas, *Summa Theologica* I, ii, I; Flew, *God and Philosophy* 2, 18–19; and pp. 31–2, above.

38. Job 37—41.
39. Matt. 5.5, Luke 6.21.
40. J. Hick, *Evil and the God of Love*, pp. 377–81.
41. Cf. *Institutes* III, 21, 5, 222.
42. *Church Dogmatics*, III, 1, 222; Gen. 1.31.
43. The relevant material has been assembled by Hick, *Evil and the God of Love*, 388–93; it is summarized in this paragraph.
44. p. 179.
45. *Religion in the Making*, 92–4.
46. ibid. 95.
47. ibid., 104.
48. I. R. Barbour, *Issues in Science and Religion*, p. 439.
49. Mackie, op. cit., p. 209.
50. Plantinga, op. cit., p. 213.
51. *Evil and the God of Love*, p. 308.
52. p. 291.
53. This paragraph is heavily indebted to Hick, op. cit., pp. 345–53.
54. e.g., 2 Peter 2.4; Jude 6. Cf. C. S. Lewis, *The Problem of Pain*; also A. Plantinga, "The Free Will Defence", in *Philosophy in America*, ed. Max Black, p. 219.
55. Malcolm, "Anselm's Ontological Arguments", in *Religion and Understanding*, ed. D. Z. Phillips, p. 48.
56. Augustine, *De Trinitate* vi, 8.
57. pp. 80–1, above.
58. pp. 74–5, above.
59. op. cit., pp. 5–6.

CHAPTER 4

1. *Enquiries*, ed. Selby-Bigge, p. 114.
2. I am indebted for the substance of this argument to the paper "Miracles" by P. H. Nowell-Smith (*New Essays in Philosophical Theology*, pp. 243–53).
3. *De Trinitate*, iii, 5.
4. Matt. 17.23–6.
5. John 11.1–44; 6.1–59; 9.1–41.
6. Matt. 8.24–5, John 2.1–10, Matt. 8.28–34, 14.15–21.
7. Cf. the discussion of Freud and Marx on pp. 22–4, above.
8. Cf. particularly *Symbols of Transformation* and *Psychology and Religion* (vols. 5 and 11 of the Collected Works).
9. *Summa Theologica* I, i, 10.
10. *Psychology and Religion*, pp. 154 f.
11. In the following paragraphs I have drawn heavily on the article in "Miracles" by J. H. Bernard in Hastings' *Dictionary of the Bible*.
12. Matt. 8.28, 15.21, 17.14; Mark 1.23.
13. Matt. 8.5, 9.2; Mark 7.32; Matt. 9.27; John 9.1, etc.; Luke 14.2; Matt. 8.2; Luke 17.12; Matt. 9.18; Luke 7.11; John 11.43.
14. Matt. 21.18, 8.26, 14.25, 15.32, 14.19; John 2.9.

15. *Interpreting the Miracles.*
16. op. cit., pp. 8 f, 10 f.
17. p. 15.
18. Matt. 21.1–13.
19. John 4.4–8.
20. For a sceptical account of the historical credibility of these narratives, cf. especially Bultmann, *The History of the Synoptic Tradition.* Among the most scholarly recent presentations of the opposite point of view is B. Gerhardsson's *Memory and Manuscript.*
21. Fuller, op. cit., pp. 11–12.
22. Cf. L. Monden, *Signs and Wonders*, p. 181.
23. "The Miraculous", in *Religion and Understanding*, ed. D. Z. Phillips, pp. 155 f.

CHAPTER 5

1. C. L. Stevenson, *Ethics and Language*, pp. 277–90.
2. In this and the following paragraphs I am indebted to the article *Prayer in the Bible*, by M. R. E. Masterman, in the *New Catholic Encyclopaedia.*
3. Psalm 25.1–4, 23.
4. Cf. Jeremiah and Job.
5. Pss. 54, 42, 67, 143.
6. Pss. 108, 94.5–6, 20.
7. Ps. 105.
8. 1 Sam. 12.10.
9. Ps. 22.25.
10. Luke 3.21, 5.16, etc.
11. Matt. 14.23.
12. John 8.29, 11.41–2.
13. Matt. 6.9–13.
14. Luke 17.5–6, Matt. 7.7–11, 6.5–8.
15. Mark 11.24.
16. Matt. 18.19–20.
17. Acts 4.29–30; Rom. 15.31–2; Eph. 18–20.
18. 1 Tim. 2.1–2, Matt. 5.44.
19. F. Heiler, *Prayer*, p. 102.
20. Jonah ii.
21. Matt. 6.9–13.
22. Cf. Matt. 7.7–11.
23. This and the following paragraph owe a great deal to chapter 7 of Professor P. T. Geach's *God and the Soul*, though my conclusions are not quite the same as his.
24. Cf. pp. 47–56, above.
25. I. Barbour, *Issues in Science and Religion*, p. 428.
26. On this matter, with some hesitation, I agree with C. S. Lewis against Professor Geach.
27. D. Z. Phillips, *The Concept of Prayer*, p. 2.

28. *Religion within the Limits of Reason Alone*, p. 181.
29. Heiler, *Prayer*, p. 356.
30. ibid., p. 355.
31. John 10.10.
32. Cf. Cicero, *De Natura Deorum*, 36. Also Lonergan, "St Thomas on *Gratia Operans*" (*Theological Studies* II, 1941, p. 290).
33. *The Concept of Prayer*, p. 95.
34. ibid., p. 17.
35. ibid., p. 148.
36. ibid., p. 10.
37. ibid., p. 150.
38. ibid., p. 38.
39. Luke 18.9–14.
40. op. cit., p. 115.
41. ibid., p. 67.
42. Aquinas, *Compendium Theologiae*, 251; cf. Gilby, *St Thomas Aquinas. Theological Texts*, pp. 205 ff.

CHAPTER 6

1. *De Mor*. Eccl. I, 27, 52; of Gilson, *The Christian Philosophy of Saint Augustine*, p. 45.
2. *De Anima*, II, 1; Aquinas, *Summa Theologica*, I, lxxvi, 1.
3. *Religion, Philosophy and Psychical Research*, pp. 234 f.
4. *The Concept of Prayer*, 34.
5. Cf. the discussion on "Death" between D. M. MacKinnon and A. G. N. Flew, in *New Essays in Philosophical Theology*, ed. Flew and MacIntyre; Flew, pp. 267–8.
6. MacKinnon, op. cit., p. 262.
7. ibid., p. 264.
8. Flew, op. cit., p. 269.
9. p. 117.
10. Flew, op. cit., p. 270.
11. Hindu theists characteristically believe in the immortality of the soul, Islamic and Zoroastrian in the resurrection of the body. The majority of Christian theists have held to both doctrines.
12. Cf. J. J. C. Smart, "Sensations and Brain Processes" (*Philosophical Review* 1959), p. 145.
13. Cf. L. Wittgenstein, *Philosophical Investigations*, I, 243 ff.
14. By Corbett Thigpen and Harvey Cleckley.
15. Flew, op. cit., p. 270.
16. A sane and lucid summary of some of the evidence is to be found in G. N. M. Tyrrell's *The Personality of Man*.
17. *Personal Survival and Psychical Research*.
18. I owe this example to some suggestions of Prof. P. T. Geach.
19. In *Gods* (Logic and Language, I, ed. Flew; 169–81).
20. Flew, op. cit., 269.

CONCLUSION

1. *Question*, January 1969.
2. p. 35.
3. p. 51.
4. p. 47 and elsewhere.
5. This is far more unambiguous in the case of Phillips than Robinson, who sometimes seems to approach closer to what I would call the traditional point of view.
6. p. 42.
7. p. 34.
8. *New Essays in Philosophical Theology*, 103–5.
9. p. 35.
10. p. 36.
11. p. 35.
12. Cf. pp. 55–6, above. A similar line of thought is developed by Peter Bertocci, in *The Person God Is* (*Talk of God*, 205).
13. p. 50.
14. p. 48.
15. p. 37.
16. p. 37.
17. pp. 37–8.
18. pp. 38–9.
19. Phillips, *The Concept of Prayer*, 32 f.
20. For all Phillips's appeal to, and often valuable commentary on, Kierkegaard and Simone Weil (Nielsen, p. 52), these thinkers are on the whole rather traditional than reductionist in my sense.

APPENDIX

1. These works will be referred to in the following notes by the initials RM, PR, SMW, and AI.
2. RM, pp. 58, 66, 60, 62.
3. RM, pp. 68 ff., 150.
4. RM, pp. 73 ff., PR, p. 484, RM, pp. 76–9.
5. SMW, pp. 88, 105, 159; PR, p. 208, etc.
6. RM, pp. 89 f., 108; PR, p. 3; RM, 94 (cf. SMW, pp. 161, 174, 178); RM, p. 104; AI, p. 146; RM, p. 153; PR, p. 43.
7. SMW, chapter 5.
8. The appendix to D. M. Emmet's *The Nature of Metaphysical Thinking* (p. 228–34) well elucidates Whitehead's thought on this topic.
9. RM, pp. 100, 103; PR, pp. 249, 169, 227, 77; RM, pp. 95 f.; PR, p. 489; RM, pp. 156, 159, 119 f., 104 f., 143.
10. RM, pp. 104 f., 99; PR, p. 43, 16 f., 147, 493 f.; cf. PR, p. 528.
11. *Summa Theologica* I, ii, 3.
12. *A Christian Natural Theology, based on the thought of Alfred North Whitehead*, p. 143.

13. For a criticism of Whitehead's solution of the problem of evil, cf. *Evil and the Concept of God*, by E. H. Madden and P. H. Hare, pp. 115–25.
14. pp. 45–8, above.
15. pp. 62–3, above.

BIBLIOGRAPHY

GENERAL

Aquinas, Thomas, *Summa Theologica*, tr. the Fathers of the English Dominican Province. London 1912.
—— *Summa Theologica*, Latin Text with English tr. by various authors. Eyre & Spottiswoode 1964–7.
—— *Texts, Philosophical and Theological*, ed. T. Gilby. Eyre & Spottiswoode 1951, 55.
Barth, K., *Church Dogmatics*. T. and T. Clark 1936, 1956.
Farmer, H. H., *The World and God*. Fontana 1963.
Flew, A. G. N., *God and Philosophy*. Hutchinson 1966.
Flew, A. G. N. and MacIntyre, A. (ed), *New Essays in Philosophical Theology*. S.C.M. 1963.[1]
Geach, P. T., *God and the Soul*. Routledge, 1969.
Hick, J., *Philosophy of Religion*. Prentice-Hall 1964.
—— *Faith and Knowledge*, 2nd ed. Macmillan 1967.
—— (ed.) *Faith and the Philosophers*. Macmillan 1964.
McPherson, T., *Philosophy of Religion*. Van Nostrand 1965.
Macquarrie, J., *Twentieth-Century Religious Thought*. S.C.M. 1966.
Mitchell, B. G., (ed.) *Faith and Logic*. Allen and Unwin 1957.
Nielsen, Kai, "Language and the Concept of God" (*Question*, Jan. 1969, 34–52).
Phillips, D. Z. (ed.), *Religion and Understanding*. Blackwell 1967.
Price, H. H., "Faith and Belief" (*Faith and the Philosophers*, ed. Hick pp. 3–25).
Ramsey, I. T., *Religious Language*. S.C.M. 1967.
Smart, N., *Philosophers and Religious Truth*. S.C.M. 1969.
—— *Reasons and Faiths*. Routledge 1958.
Tillich, P., *Systematic Theology*, Vols. 1, 2, and 3. Nisbet 1953, 1957, and 1964.
Vesey, G. N. A. (and others), *Talk of God*. London 1969.

[1] Referred to as NEPT in the rest of the bibliography.

INTRODUCTION

Ayer, A. J., *Language, Truth and Logic* (especially chapter 6). Gollancz 1946.
Bambrough, R. (with R. W. Hepburn *et al.*), *Religion and Humanism*. BBC 1964.
Braithwaite, R. B., *An Empiricist's View of the Nature of Religious Belief*. Cambridge University Press 1955.

Bartsch, H. W. (ed.), *Kerygma and Myth*, Vols. 1 and 2. S.P.C.K. 1953 and 1962.
van Buren, P., *The Secular Meaning of the Gospel*. Penguin 1968.
Jung, C. G., *Psychology and Religion*. Collected Works, Vol. 2. Routledge 1958.

CHAPTER 1

Barbour, I. G., *Issues in Science and Religion*. S.C.M. 1966.
Bartley, W. W., *The Retreat to Commitment*. Chatto and Windus 1964.
Birch, L. C., *Nature and God*. S.C.M. 1965.
Braithwaite, R. B., Dialogue between Richard and Gregory (*Theoria to Theory*, Autumn 1966, pp. 44–54).
Brown, Patterson, St. Thomas's Doctrine of Necessary Being; *Philosophical Review*, 1964, 76–90.
Coval, S., Worship, Superlatives and Concept Confusion, *Mind*, 1959, 218–22.
Crombie, I. M., Contribution to symposium *Theology and Falsification;* NEPT, 109–30.
Farrer, A. M., Finite and Infinite. Dacre Press 1943.
Findlay, J. N., "Can God's Existence be Disproved?"; NEPT, 47–56, 71–5.
Flew, A. G. N., Contribution to symposium *Theology and Falsification*. NEPT, 96–9, 106–8.
Freud, S., *Civilisation and its Discontents*. Hogarth Press, 1930.
—— *The Future of an Illusion*. Hogarth Press 1928.
Geach, P. T. (with Anscombe, G. E. M.), *Three Philosophers*. Blackwell 1961.
Gilson, E., *The Philosophy of St. Thomas Aquinas*. Gollancz 1961.
Hare, R. M., Contribution to symposium *Theology and Falsification*; NEPT, 99–103.
Hepburn, R. W., *Christianity and Paradox*. Watts 1958. A Critique of Humanist Theology (*Objections to Humanism*, ed. H. J. Blackham. Constable 1963; 29–54).
Hick, J., *Theology's Central Problem*. Birmingham University 1967.
Hudson, W. D., "An Attempt to Defend Theism"; *Philosophy*, 1964, 18–28.
Hume, D., Dialogues concerning Natural Religion (*Hume, Selections*, ed. C. W. Hendel. Scribner 1955), 284–401.
—— *Enquiries*; ed. L. A. Selby-Bigge. Oxford 1902; especially chapter 11 of the First Enquiry.
Kant, I., *Critique of Pure Reason*, tr. J. M. D. Meiklejohn. Everyman 1934.
—— *Religion within the Limits of Reason Alone*, tr. T. M. Greene and H. H. Hudson. Harper & Brothers 1960.
Kierkegaard, S., *Philosophical Fragments*, tr. D. Swenson. Princeton University Press 1962.
Lewis, H. D., *Our Experience of God*. Allen and Unwin 1959.

Lonergan, B. J. F., *Insight: a Study of Human Understanding*. Longmans 1957.
MacIntyre, A. C., "Is Understanding Religion Compatible with Believing?" (*Faith and the Philosophers*, ed. Hick, 115–33).
—— The Logical Status of Religious Belief (*Metaphysical Beliefs* ed. MacIntyre. London 1957), 169–211.
Malcolm, N., "Anselm's Ontological Arguments"; *Philosophical Review*, 1960, also in *Religion and Understanding*, ed. Phillips, 43–61.
Marx, K., (and Engels, F.), *On Religion*. Foreign languages Publishing House, Moscow 1957.
Meynell, H. A., *Sense, Nonsense and Christianity*. Sheed and Ward 1964.
Mitchell, B. G., Contribution to symposium *Theology and Falsification;* NEPT, 103–5.
—— "The Justification of Religious Belief"; *Philosophical Quarterly*, 1961, 213–26.
Munz, P., *Problems of Religious Knowledge*. S.C.M. 1959.
Phillips, D. Z., Philosophy, Theology and the Reality of God; *Philosophical Quarterly*, 1963, 344–50.
Ross, J. F., "God and 'Logical Necessity'"; *Philosophical Quarterly*, 1961, 22–7.
Stace, W. T., *Mysticism and Philosophy*. Macmillan 1961.
Swinburne, R. G., The Argument from Design; *Philosophy*, 1968, 199–211.
Taylor, A. E., Theism (article in Hastings' *Encyclopaedia of Religion and Ethics*. Clark 1908–26).
Velecky, L. C., "Flew on Aquinas"; *Philosophy* 1968, 212–30.
Wisdom, J., Gods (*Philosophy and Psychoanalysis*. Blackwell 1964, 149–68).

CHAPTER 2

Adams, M. McC., "Is the Existence of God a 'Hard' Fact?"; *Philosophical Review*, 1967, 492–503.
Augustine, *On the City of God* (tr. J. Healey); 2 vols. Everyman 1945.
Calvin, J., *Institutes of the Christian Religion*; tr. H. Beveridge. Clarke 1962.
Chisholm, R., "Responsibility and Avoidability" (*Determinism and Freedom in the Age of Modern Science*, ed. S. Hook. Collier Books 1961), 157–9.
Edwards, J., *Freedom of the Will*. Yale University Press 1957.
Gallie, W. B., "Explanation in History and in the Genetic Sciences"; *Mind*, 1955, 160–80).
Kneale, W., "Time and Eternity in Theology"; *Proceedings of the Aristotelian Society*, 1961.
Lonergan, B. J. F., "St Thomas's Thought on *Gratia Operans*"; *Theological Studies*, 1941, 289–324; 1942, 69–88, 375–402, 533–78.
Mitchell, B. G., "The Grace of God"; *Faith and Logic*, ed. Mitchell, 149–75.

Pike, N., "Divine Omniscience and Voluntary Action"; *Philosophical Review*, 1965. 27–46.
Prior, A. N., "The Formalities of Omniscience"; *Philosophy*, 1962, 114–129.

CHAPTER 3

Hick, J., *Evil and the God of Love*. Macmillan 1966.
Leibniz, G. W., *Theodicy*; tr. E. M. Huggard. Routledge 1951.
Lewis, C. S., *The Problem of Pain*. Centenary Press 1940.
Mackie, J. R., "Evil and Omnipotence"; *Mind*, 1955, 200–12.
Madden, E. H., *Evil and the Concept of God*. Charles Thomas 1968 (with Hare, P. H.)
Pike, N., "Hume on Evil"; *Philosophical Review*, 1963, 180–97.
Plantinga, A., "The Free Will Defence"; *Philosophy in America*, ed. Max Black. (Allen & Unwin 1965), 204–20.
Puccetti, R., "The Concept of God"; *Philosophical Quarterly*, 1964, 237–45.
Smart, N., "Omnipotence, Evil, and Supermen"; *Philosophy*, 1961, 188–95.

CHAPTER 4

Fuller, R. H., *Interpreting the Miracles*. S.C.M. 1963.
Hume, D., *Enquiries* (Chapter X of First Enquiry); ed. L. A. Selby-Bigge. Oxford University Press 1902.
Lewis, C. S., *Miracles*. Centenary Press 1947.
Monden, L. *Signs and Wonders*. Desclée 1966.
Moule, C. F. D. (ed.), *Miracles: Cambridge Studies in their Philosophy and History*. Mowbray 1965.
Nowell-Smith, P. H., Miracles; NEPT, 243–53.

CHAPTER 5

von Balthasar, H. U., *Prayer*. Chapman, 1963.
Bloom, A., *Living Prayer*. Darton, Longman, & Todd 1966.
Cant, R., *Christian Prayer*. Faith Press, 1961.
Hamman, A., *La Prière*; 1959, 1963.
Heiler, F., *Prayer*; Oxford University Press 1932.
Northcott, H., *The Venture of Prayer*. S.P.C.K. 1950.
Phillips, D. Z., *The Concept of Prayer*. Routledge 1965.

CHAPTER 6

Broad, C. D., *Religion, Philosophy and Psychical Research*. Routledge 1953.
—— *Personal Identity and Survival*. Society for Psychological Research, 1958.
Flew, A. G. N., Contribution to symposium *Death*; NEPT, 261–72.

Gustafson, D. F., (ed.) *Essays in Philosophical Psychology*. Doubleday 1964.
Lucas, J. R., "The Soul"; *Faith and Logic*, ed. B. Mitchell, 132–48.
MacKinnon, D. M., Contribution to symposium *Death*; NEPT, 261–72.
Ryle, G., *The Concept of Mind*. Hutchinson's University Library 1949.
Shaffer, J., "Persons and their Bodies"; *Philosophical Review*, 1966, 59–77.
Shoemaker, S. *Self-knowledge and Self-Identity*. Cornell University Press 1963.
Smart, J. J. C., "Sensations and Brain Processes"; *Philosophical Review*, 1959, 141–56.
Stevenson, J. T., "Reply to J. J. C. Smart"; *Philosophical Review*, 1960, 505–10.
Wittgenstein, L., *Philosophical Investigations*. Blackwell 1958.

APPENDIX

Cobb, J. B., *A Christian Natural Theology, based on the thought of Alfred North Whitehead*. Lutterworth 1966.
Emmett, D. M., *The Nature of Metaphysical Thinking*. Macmillan 1945. (especially the Appendix).
Whitehead, A. N., *Adventures of Ideas*. Cambridge University Press 1933.
—— *Process and Reality*. Cambridge University Press, 1929.
—— *Religion in the Making*. Cambridge University Press, 1926.
—— *Science and the Modern World*. Mentor Books, 1948.

INDEX

Anselm, 134
apologetics, 2
Aquinas, 11, 13–16, 19, 31–2, 44, 59–60, 62, 67–70, 87, 110–11, 124, 132–3
arguments for existence of God, 10–12, 24–5, 135
Aristotle, 13–14, 111–12, 115
Ashby, W. R., 13, 15–16
astrology, 3
Augustine, 32, 56, 59, 67–8, 79–80, 85, 96, 111
Ayer, A. J., 114, 136

Bambrough, R., 136
Bañez, 57–8
Barbour, I. R., 78
Barth, K., 9–10, 34, 64–5, 77, 124, 135
Bartley, W. W., 34
Bernard, J. H., 140
Bertocci, P., 143
Boethius, 62, 104
Braithwaite, R. B., 5–8
Broad, C. D., 112, 120
Buddhism, 1, 88
Bultmann, R., 4–5, 7–8, 28, 30, 39, 43, 89, 124, 136, 142
van Buren, P., 6

Calvin, J., 48–9, 56–7, 60–1
Catullus, 66
Chisholm, R., 49–51, 53
Cobb, J. B., 132
Crombie, I., 35–6
cybernetics, 13–15

Descartes, R., 10
determinism, 47–56, 104, 138
Dickens, C., 45

Eccles, J. C., 138
Edwards, J., 60–2
Einstein, A., 16
Emmet, D. M., 143
empiricism, 25–6

fact and value, 5, 7, 37
faith and reason, 39–40
Findlay, J. H., 20
Flew, A. G. N., 16–18, 27–34, 75, 121, 142
Freud, S., 23–4, 44–5, 135
Fuller, R. H., 91–2

Geach, P. T., 141–2
Gerhardsson, B., 141
Gnosticism, 106
goodness of God, 49, 64, 70, 75–8, 81–2, 132–3

Hare, P. H., 144
Hare, R. M., 137
Hartshorne, C., 60–1
Hegel, 127
Heidegger, M., 22, 43
Heiler, F., 141
Hepburn, R. W., 136
Hick, J., 67–8, 79, 83, 140
Hinduism, 1, 44, 88, 106, 142
Hobbes, T., 30, 60
Hollard, R. F., 96–7
Hoyle, F., 18
Hudson, D., 136–7
Hume, D., 14, 24, 30, 51–2, 84–5, 93, 96, 98, 125, 131
Huxley, J., 25

intercession, 108
Islam, 25, 44, 56, 130, 142

Jainism, 1

Job, 76
John, St, 42, 74, 85–6, 107, 130
Jung, C. G., 6–8, 87–8

Kant, E., 11–12, 50, 105–6
Karma, 33
Kierkegaard, S., 38–9, 142

Lewis, C. S., 140–1
Lonergan, B., 124

McCabe, H., 32, 43
Mackie, J. L., 71–5, 79
MacKinnon, D. M., 139, 142
Madden, E. H., 144
magic, 103–4
Malcolm, N., 81, 140
Marx, K., 23–4, 43–5
Masterman, M. R. E., 141
meaning of terms predicated of God, 20–1, 29–32
Milligan, M., 138
Mitchell, B., 124, 137
Molina, 57–8, 136
Moltmann, J., 138
Monden, L., 141
multiple personality, 116–17
myth, 86–8

nature, 14–18, 84–5, 92–3, 96–7
necessary existence, 19–20
Nielsen, K., 122–8
Nowell-Smith, P. H., 93, 95, 140

omnipotence, 21, 71–2, 78–9
Origen, 48
original sin, 44

pantheism, 18–19
paradox and contradiction, 66
Pascal, B., 19
Paul, St, 37, 42, 56, 106
Pelagius, 56–7, 60
personal identity, 113–19
persuasive definition, 98
petition, 102–5
Phillips, D. Z., 37, 98, 108–10, 112, 122–8, 143
Plantinga, A., 79
Plato, 55, 111–12, 115, 130
Pollard, W., 104
poltergeists, 55–6
Popper, K., 34, 135
private languages, 116
"profound truth", 88
providence, 60
psychical research, 119–20

Rahner, K., 44, 124, 138
reasons and causes, 54–5
reductionist theism, 123, 126–7
reincarnation, 117–18
religious experience, 21–2
Robinson, H. W., 136
Robinson, J. A. T., 13, 122–8, 135, 143
Ryle, G., 135

sacraments, 45
Schleiermacher, F., 127, 136
science, 2, 85, 96, 122
secularism, 45
Shankara, 1
sin, 30, 42–5, 57–60, 69–70, 77–9
Smart, J. J. C., 136
Smart, N., 74–5
Stevenson, C. L., 98
Stoicism, 108

Teilhard de Chardin, 47
Thurston, R., 138
Tillich, P., 30–1, 34, 43–4, 125, 136–7
transcendence, 16–17, 132
Tyrrell, G. N. M., 142

verification and falsification, 33, 39–40, 124

Weil, S., 143
Whitehead, A. N., 78, 129–33
Williams, B., 124
Wisdom, J., 120–1
Wittgenstein, L., 3

Zoroastrianism, 142